Michael Divilly

20 - Jun - 78

Plain Sailing

An Introductory Guide

Bill Beavis

Based on the Yorkshire Television Series

Stanley Paul, London

Stanley Paul & Co Ltd
3 Fitzroy Square, London W1P 6JD

An imprint of the Hutchinson Publishing Group

London Melbourne Sydney Auckland
Wellington Johannesburg and agencies
throughout the world

First Published January 1976
Second impression May 1976
© Trident International Television
Enterprises Ltd, 1976

Set in Monotype Times and Univers

Printed in Great Britain by The Anchor Press Ltd
and bound by Wm Brendon & Son Ltd
both of Tiptree, Essex

ISBN 0 09 125730 1 (cased)
     0 09 125731 x (paper)

CONTENTS

INTRODUCTION

Plain Sailing represents most of what I know about sailing for beginners. In presenting it, however, I am so well aware of the variety and diversity of conditions at sea that I would not pretend this book could be complete and accurate for every occasion.

Every occasion, obviously, is unique, and once you have set off along the right lines (which is my intention) then experience will later teach you how the information in this book may be adapted to cope with the vagaries of boats and the sea. The purpose of this book, then, is to provide a fundamental introduction. It can show you how and where to begin, and what sort of sailing there is to be had; it tells you how to determine what class of boat will best suit you and how to get a boat of your own; and it gives you the essential principles of sailing – those which are common to all boats and all situations.

Read it in conjunction with an evening course in navigation, before a summer sailing school, or between trips in someone else's boat. Or, since I must point out that you ought to learn to swim and life-save before you start, read it on the way to the swimming baths.

But whatever you do, please do not imagine that the learning stops on the last page – for at that stage you are just about to begin in earnest.

1 BEGINNINGS

Sadly, most of the stunts have been done. You need something really outstanding to attract a sponsor's eye: a mother-in-law prepared to ride the Blue Nile on an inflated hippo skin; a dog who will sail backwards in the next trans-Atlantic. And unless you can come up with something original like this, then boating, you will find, is expensive!

It also makes a disproportionate demand on your energies and time; in fact if you add it all up, compare what you have to put in to what you get out, you'll find that mile for mile, the American moon shot was only marginally more expensive.

Furthermore it's uncomfortable and very much as somebody once described: 'like standing under a cold shower tearing up five pound notes'. Not that you'll mind the expense when sailing gets a hold on you. The money will come from somewhere and you will lavish it on your new sport as compulsively as you already do DIY jobs around the house, or your wife and children's clothing (and there are two likely sources for you).

But meanwhile before you reach this euphoric state you will want to sample the sport to see whether you are going to like it. There is of course nothing to stop you rushing out and buying a boat, that is to say no licences, tests and suchlike. But how much more sensible to start in someone else's boat, tear up someone else's five pound notes!

Like all *sensible* suggestions, sailing in another person's boat is never so exciting as setting off in one of your own; that's a completely different experience. And particularly in a sport like sailing where a large part of the pleasure comes from freedom and self-achievement (beautiful sentiment: most people it happens to are too numb scared to feel anything!).

However, your first few trips in another person's boat will probably be disappointing. For no matter how patient and long-suffering the owner and his companions may be it is inevitable

5

that you will feel clumsy and burdensome. And things happen so quickly. A word, which could be Portuguese, rings out. A rope is pulled, another is freed while the crew, with the exception of you, all move about the boat like demons.

You're not entirely sure what's happening but suspect they're trying to kill you. A deadly-looking piece of wood swishes just an inch above your head and the place where they told you to sit suddenly slides down to the water. Even the scenery changes; the movement is different; it's noisier; the sun goes in and whereas you were warm and comfortable before, now you are wet and shaking. And all this just when you thought you were beginning to enjoy it.

Finally when the frenzy is over a suntanned gorilla of a man sitting next to you takes pity. He leans over and kindly and clearly explains the movements and the principle of what has just been happening. He speaks in Portuguese. However, you smile timidly back from under the hood of your oilskin, produce the rope he told you to hold half an hour ago and ask: 'Is it all right to let go now?' A little while later you are seasick.

Now it could be that you started out on the wrong foot; fell in with the wrong sort of companions, sailed in the wrong sort of boat. Or it could be that you really have chosen the wrong sport and would be happier in the garden growing competition marrows. But don't give up yet because the pleasure that comes with sailing is something which has to be worked for. Oh sure it's very nice to do the boating 'things'; lounge on a deck in the sun; swim in your birthday suit; share sunsets with the marsh birds; sing shanties by the light of an oil lamp; go without washing or shaving – but these are just incidentals. The real enjoyment and satisfaction comes when the things you have learned are mastered and put into practice, when through your judgement and skill you make your boat go faster than the rest, or when you can confidently take her out over the horizon and bring her safely into a new harbour, and when you finally triumph over fears and put yourself to the test. No amount of cold, damp weather and physical discomfort can dull the satisfaction that brings you.

All right then, but how does one start? Well it would probably surprise you to know that at any major yachting centre, on any summer weekend, there are literally hundreds of boats harbour-bound because their owners cannot find a crew to sail with them. And before that brings to mind notions of Captain Bligh, weevils and walking the plank, let me put in straight away that there are still more boats sailing with happy, contented crews who would gladly make room for you. In short there are plenty of places to fill, it is merely a matter of making contact.

Now if you live in a flat in Solihull and the only connections you have with the sea are a jar of winkles and a grandfather who fought at Jutland, you would probably consider that a glib and insensitive remark. But the fact is that nobody minds shipping a raw beginner. Sailing is not such a serious sport and there are not that many sailing people who you might describe as 'dedicated to winning'. Sailing is a sociable thing, a matter of getting along together, and providing you appear keen, cheerful and ready to work then you'll be as welcome aboard as flowers in spring. Of course it's no good being chirpy, keen and industrious and turning up with a tin trunk, a pair of hob-nailed boots and a face covered with contagious-looking pimples; that would tend to weigh against you. But then the purpose of the first part of this book is to 'school' you so that you will know what is expected of you and hopefully have a little knowledge to offer.

Drive down to your nearest sailing centre one Saturday and talk to as many people as you can. Boatyard managers, Harbour Masters and their staff – sailing club secretaries are particularly helpful. Explain to them that you are anxious to get afloat, that you are prepared to work and pay your way and might they know of anybody who could offer you a berth in their boat for a season? If you can arrange your visit in the early spring so much the better. This is when boats are customarily fitted out; find an owner struggling against time and the elements and offer your help and you are practically guaranteed a regular sail during the season. In fact he'll probably throw his arms round your neck. There are hundreds who are happy to go sailing all summer but they vanish like holiday camp cutlery when there is work to be done in the winter.

Failing this you might study the small ads of a magazine such as *Yachting Monthly*, where there are never less than a dozen 'crews looking for owners' or 'owners looking for crews' (some under *Personal*, some under *Lost and Found*).

But it could be that despite wading through the chapters of this book you still come out the other end not knowing one part of a boat from another – no matter. Perhaps you have a thorough knowledge of engines, or electronics, or you can cook, or speak French? Well then these are your 'trading' qualities. Ask the sailing club secretary to put them on the club notice-board along with your name and telephone number, go home, and wait for the phone calls. If the owner of a cruising boat needs help with anything more than fitting out – it's his engine, his cooking and his French.

So far the advice has been primarily directed at the single man or woman, sailing in what will, of necessity, be a large and probably uncompetitive boat. Obviously this is no help for the man who wishes to go afloat with his family. An owner might be prepared to pick up *one* novice but he is hardly likely to ship a whole family of novices.

Then again, getting afloat either by making yourself indispensable, or by ingratiation isn't going to be much help to the youngster who wishes to take up dinghy sailing. He or she has not yet acquired the crafts and skills of a grown-up, nor any of their smooth manoeuvrings.

It is usually at this juncture that the beginner is told to go and join a yacht club. An unhelpful, unsympathetic remark that is magically supposed to sort you out (a hundred years ago the same haughty voice was advising a few nights in Paris or a cold bath). Certainly if a beginner can join a yacht club then his needs will be well attended, but how are you supposed to get proposed, seconded and elected when you don't know anyone there in the first place? And it is true that some of the established clubs can appear a little forbidding – like a Beirut night club might be to the secretary of a boys' club. Besides they will likely be already over-subscribed so your whispered confidence 'Joe sent me' won't hold much sway with the wing-collared flunkey on the door.

It is unwise to generalize but you may find that some of the 'Portakabin' yacht clubs that have sprung up over the past few years will be better able to take on new members. They generally need support and what they lack in foundations and frontage they make up in friendliness and informality. More-

8

over they are cheaper to join and if you are able to offer any special skills, such as a knowledge of plumbing or the legal system, then you are certain to be accepted. Seem to have a lot of trouble with the council and drainage these places.

Up until a few years ago the described method of winkling your way in was the only way, short of actually stealing a boat or joining the Navy, that you could hope to pick up any experience. Nowadays it is different. Hundreds of sailing schools have mushroomed where you and your family can spend a week or a fortnight being taught how to sail and pay little more than you would for a continental holiday. Most of these schools are affiliated to the Royal Yachting Association, which inspects and satisfies itself that the instruction given is to an approved standard. In many of the schools also, students can take one or other of the several RYA certificate courses which are designed to meet, respectively, the needs of a dinghy sailor, a cruising man or a person who eventually wishes to sail in a teaching capacity in a large sailing ship. The schools provide most of the practical teaching required to meet the standards of these certificates, but candidates will also be required to take an evening course on subjects such as seamanship and navigation (and here is a good opportunity to meet someone who owns a boat). For a complete list of 'approved' schools and for details of the training schemes write to the RYA. You'll find their address in the list of Useful Addresses.

Another method of receiving training afloat is by chartering a boat with a professional skipper. Many such charter firms are advertised in the yachting magazines although you would be advised to apply to those that specifically state 'tuition'.

There are also opportunities to get afloat by joining the Island Cruising Club or the Ocean Youth Club or similar associations. The former is the forerunner of an imaginative scheme whereby the members actually own the boats – they each buy a small share with their subscriptions, and run sail-training holidays for themselves. The club does employ a small professional staff, but it exists largely on the voluntary labour and support of its many members.

To summarize then, there are very many ways in which you can pick up your sea experience cheaply, it is simply a matter of giving yourself a push.

2 COMING TO TERMS

There was a captain of the old *Queen Mary* who, it was said, kept a notebook locked away in his drawer. Each morning he would go to his drawer, open the notebook and study it. He did this right up until the day he retired when he left the notebook behind. There was only one entry when they found it; it said – 'port is left, right is starboard'.

Landsmen especially can have trouble with sea terms; they probably see it as a cult language or an 'in' way of speaking specially dreamed up to exclude them. But no affectation was ever intended, for the language of the sea is a functional means of communication with its origins stretching back over centuries. The words are good, solid Saxon and you'll have no difficulty in learning them. So then on a wild and stormy night when the skipper screams, 'Stand by the boom vang I'm going to gybe her . . .' you'll know in an instant what to do . . . (pick up your phrase-book and ask him please to repeat it).

All boats are *shes*. Nobody quite knows why they are or where the directive came from. Maybe it has something to do with a similarity in temperament; maybe it's their beauty. Or maybe it is simply a sad expression of how lonely a sailor's life can be. Pretty thought isn't it? Across the Channel in France boats are masculine.

The front part of a boat is the *bows* or *fore-part* and if we walk in this direction we are said to be going *forward*. If we walk towards the back of the boat we are *going aft* and the area here is the *stern* or *after-part*. Anything which lies further aft of an object is said to be *abaft* and if it is in front then it is said to be *forward of*.

Provided we keep safely within the boat we are *aboard*; if we jump off and into the sea we are *overboard*. These terms are distinct from *outboard* and *inboard*, which although they may imply the same are generally used in connection with objects;

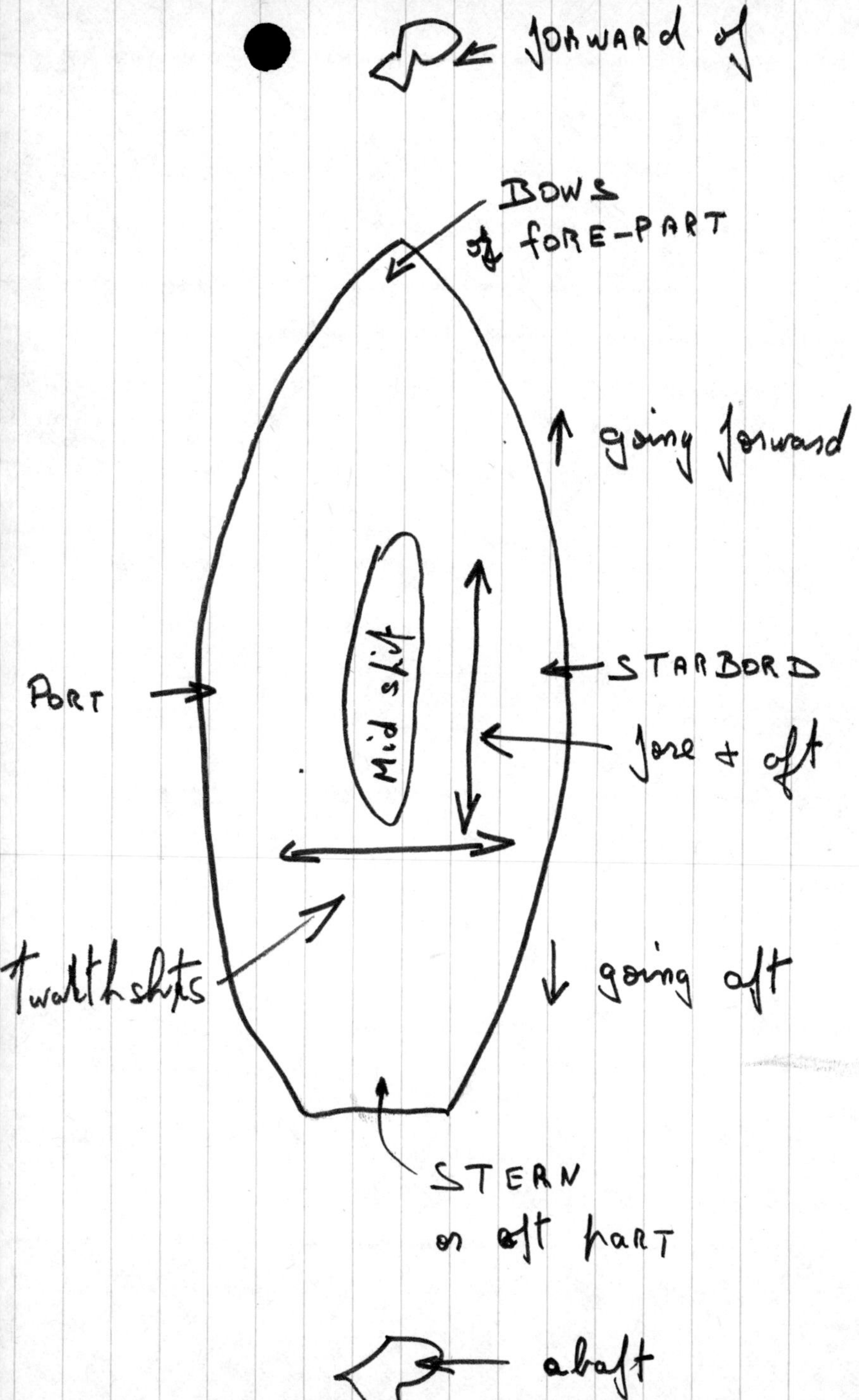

FORWARD of

BOWS
or FORE-PART

↑ going forward

Mid ship

PORT →

← STARBORD

fore & aft

← going aft ↓

Twart ships

STERN
or aft part

abaft

thus a rope trailing in the water could be said to have an *outboard* end and an *inboard* end. You could not say this of a person.

There is no upstairs and downstairs in a boat, you are either *up top* or *down below*, while anything in the mast or rigging is *aloft*.

The *port* side of the boat is on the left when you face forward (remember this because port has the same number of letters as left); the *starboard* side is on the right. The middle of the boat is the *midship* part and anything that runs across the boat from side to side is said to be *athwartships*. The seats in a dinghy run athwartships, hence the name *thwarts*. Anything at right angles to this, running down the length of the boat, is *fore and aft*.

Since boats don't run on railway lines it is clear that dangers can come from any number of different directions: another boat for example crossing her bow, or a fast ship coming up from behind her. It is for this reason, and also for the purpose of navigation, that you as the crew when reporting an object will need to name its proper direction. On the left-hand side of figure 1 there are listed a number of terms in use for this purpose; however, it will be a great help, particularly at night when sighting a distant light, if you can fix it with a more precise *bearing*. The old compass-point notation is used which divides the horizon up into thirty-two segments. This means that there are eight segments or *points* to each quadrant and it is by their quadrants that they are known. Thus an object could be described as being *four points on the starboard bow, three points abaft the port beam* and so on. Each point is in fact $11\frac{1}{4}$ degrees, but this is not so fiddlesome as it sounds, because as was so often the case with our untidy, pre-decimal system, it's a measure that relates to something quite simple and basic. A compass point is just about equal to the span of your hand when it's held out at arm's length, so to establish the bearing of an object on the bow you simply 'step' it out in hand widths. (Close one eye if it helps you.)

Distance is given in miles and cables. A cable's length is one tenth of a sea mile or roughly 200 metres. But distance at sea is hard for the beginner to judge so it would be safer to suggest that the object is either near, or a long way off!

11

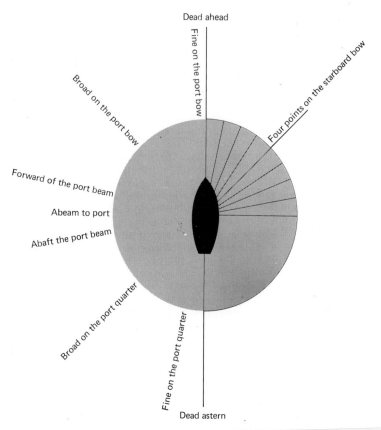

Fig 1 Directional terms

Just as a horse *trots, gallops, shies* at a gate and *unseats* its rider so there are specific terms for all boat movements. A boat when she is not made fast to the shore, at anchor or secured to a buoy, is said to be *under way*. Be careful of this term because a boat can be stopped in the water and yet still be under way. When she moves forward through the water she is then said to be *making way*. If she moves in reverse she is making a *sternboard*.

If she leans to the wind she is said to be *heeled*. But if the lean becomes permanent, i.e. through a shift in weights or by leaking water, then she is *listing*. A boat which leans easily to the wind is described as being *tender* while a boat which requires a great force of wind to heel her is said to be *stiff*. A boat is *on an even*

12

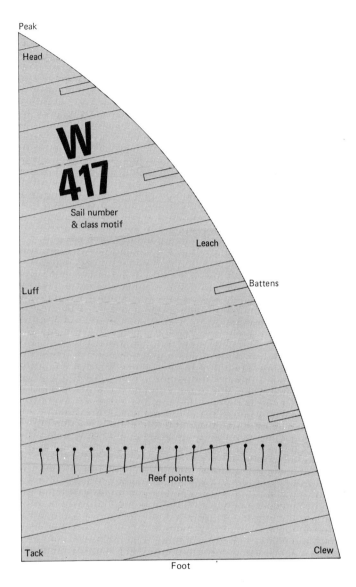

Peak

Head

W
417

Sail number
& class motif

Leach

Luff

Battens

Reef points

Tack

Clew

Foot

Fig 2 **Parts of a sail**

keel when she is level in the fore and aft line. If her bow dips she is said to be *trimmed by the head* and if her stern drops she is *trimmed by the stern.*

In a seaway a boat *rolls* from side to side and *pitches* in the fore and aft plane. If she pitches so heavily that the underpart

13

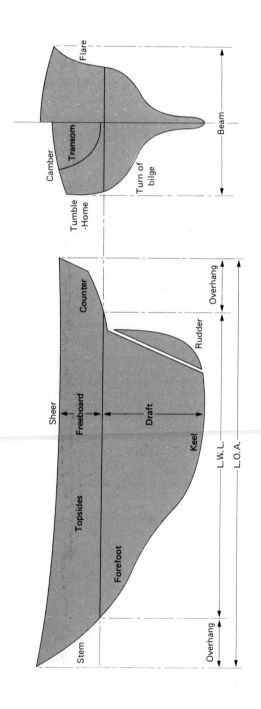

Fig 3 Descriptive terms of the hull

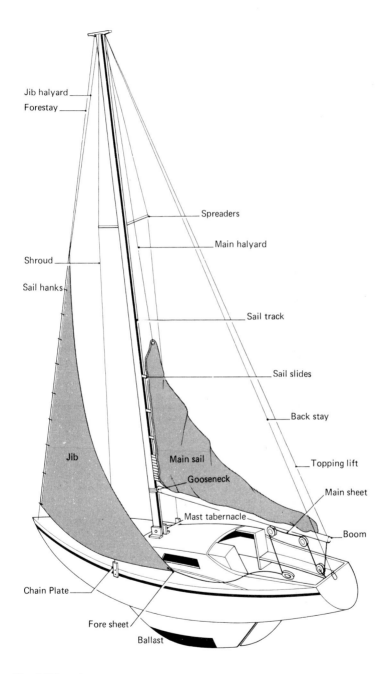

Jib halyard

Forestay

Spreaders

Main halyard

Shroud

Sail hanks

Sail track

Sail slides

Back stay

Jib

Main sail

Topping lift

Gooseneck

Main sheet

Mast tabernacle

Boom

Chain Plate

Fore sheet

Ballast

Fig 4 **The rig**

of her bow slaps the water with a jolt she is said to be *pounding* (an unhappy state which should be avoided). If, from the effect of the waves pushing against her stern, the boat's course becomes wild and erratic she is said to be *yawing*. There are many more terms in connection with handling the boat under sail but these are covered in the chapter on sailing.

The open space where the helmsman and crew sit is called the *cockpit* and the helmsman steers the boat with a *tiller* (unless it's a wheel). The raised edge of the cockpit sides are called *coamings* and the deck on which they stand is the cockpit *sole*.

If the top of the cabin or deck house is raised to give better access or more headroom then this structure is called the *doghouse*. The large opening and ladder, if there is one, are together called the *companionway*. Down below, the walls which run athwartships and help to strengthen the boat are called *bulkheads*. The roof is called the *deckhead*, the floor is the cabin *sole*, the kitchen is the *galley* and the toilet is the *heads*.

Now let's look at the sticks and strings that drive the boat along. The ropes that hoist and lower the sails are called *halyards*, the ropes that trim the sails are called *sheets*. Collectively sheets and halyards are known as the boat's *running rigging*. The wires that hold the mast upright are called the *standing rigging* and these comprise a *fore stay* and a *back stay* and *shrouds* on either side. The standing rigging is fixed to the hull with chain plates and to the mast with *vangs*. The . . . but that's enough for the time being surely!

3 GETTING A BOAT OF YOUR OWN

It is a natural inclination, when beginning a new enterprise, to start with something small and work up. It happens with yachting also but it is far from being the general rule. The climb from the small dinghy to the ocean voyager isn't necessarily a natural progression even if you are able to afford it. For each offers a very different kind of sailing, so remote in fact that if participants of both were introduced, you would find that they probably wouldn't bother to speak to each other.

If the reasons for this are not clear to you yet, they will become so, but in the meantime let it be stated that if your fancy is for a boat that you can live in then don't feel you must start with a dinghy – they're a different branch of the family. And quite apart from personal fancies, dinghies do tend to be for the more juvenile members; sailing is a healthy exercise but to hang limp and dripping – like laundry on a foggy day – from a mast trapeze is not recommended for the over sixties – brings on your twinges!

Now, having said that, we turn right about face and fling out the statistic that half the people who are sailing big boats today started with a dinghy. Why? Well for most people it is the obvious step. The dinghy, they feel, is small enough to handle, it takes little looking after, it doesn't need a mooring, it is comparatively cheap to buy and that means, if it should turn out that they don't like sailing, that it wasn't such a crippling investment.

Furthermore you learn to sail more quickly and perhaps more competently in a dinghy. It is more responsive, and sensitive, to every movement of wind and wave, to crew weight and helm and sail adjustment. Similarly all movements are quicker than they would be in a larger boat and this teaches you to make decisions rapidly. In many ways dinghy sailing gives a greater satisfaction because your skill and mastery brings the immediate

reward of feeling the boat go faster. Of course the same satisfaction can be got from larger boats too, but not to the same
intensity.

Let us suppose then that you have decided that your first
boat will be a dinghy; what type of dinghy should you look
for? Obviously it's a little premature to consider some of the
out and out racing machines on the market, which anyway
tend to be expensive and require not only an experienced
helmsman but an experienced crew member as well. Something
nearer the style of the riding stable horse, is probably the thing
to go for. Steady and safe, who, while docile in the main, is at
least fast on his way home to the stable.

The clinker-built knockabout dinghies of the pre- and early
post-war era were probably the best trainer dinghies. They were
stoutly constructed, could take a lot of punishment, were hard
to turn over and could carry a small family in reasonable
comfort. Today there are few of them left and apart from being
scarce they do have the drawback that as heavy boats they
cannot so easily be trailed from one place to another. The first
dinghy – and all those that succeed it – should be light enough
to trail to the water whether this be a beach, a river, a gravel
pit or an estuary. Even perhaps to a lake deep in the forest,
because some new owners can be strangely shy about learning.

A good dinghy to begin with is the Mirror, which was promo-
ted by the *Daily Mirror* as a sailing dinghy. You can buy the
boat new or save a few pounds by having the kit-built version
or even begin with the wood and a set of plans. Since its introduction in 1963 something like 48000 Mirror dinghies have been
launched to make it the second most popular boat in the world.

But perhaps you would like to make some open water
passages, something for which the Mirror is hardly suitable. In
which case a boat such as the Wayfarer might be your ideal.
It's a tough, proven dinghy in which many coastal passages
have been made. Moreover it is a boat in which you can
camp – that is to say sleep rough under a canvas cover or even
pull the boat ashore and pitch a tent.

It was stated earlier that half the people sailing bigger boats
today began with a dinghy. Looked at in one way this is a
fine recommendation for dinghies; looked at another way it
means they grew discontented, enough anyway to move on to

One of the most popular home-built boats in the world – the Mirror Dinghy.

something larger. People generally move to a larger boat for one of two reasons: (a) they grow older and demand more comfort, and (b) as they grow older they have families and they certainly demand more comfort.

Children can restrict sailing quite considerably – just as ably as they do other parental pleasures. But more particularly they restrict open boat sailing. They cannot, for example, be taken in a dinghy at a very tender age although many a babe in arms has sailed around in a cruiser – some have even been born in them! Indeed they shouldn't be in a dinghy at all until they are able to swim, or at least have overcome any fears by splashing around with buoyancy aids or arm-bands. Furthermore it is easier to entertain a small child aboard a larger boat than it is in a dinghy, where to add to its misery its movements are curtailed by harness and lifeline that one or other of the parents must tether. It is possible to sail dinghies with small children but the parents have to take extra care or will probably need an extra hand to sail the boat while mother loooks fter them They will have to limit their sailing to just a few hours at a time. Most people finally throw in the towel and opt for a larger boat.

But how big a boat and what kind of boat will they need? Do they still wish to race, limit their activities to day sailing, or do they want to enjoy another kind of pleasure that boating affords which is the freedom and solitude of making their home aboard – albeit only for a weekend?

For the young family man who still enjoys competition, would like to take his family afloat and perhaps make a few coastal passages, then aboat like the Squib is a very good choice. This is the intermediate step between dinghy racing and cruiser racing. The boat has nearly all the performance of a dinghy and some of the sea-going facility of a cruiser; she cannot for example be capsized. This is because she depends for her stability on the ballast of her keel and her hull shape rather than the weight of her crew which is so critical in a dinghy. The more she is heeled by the wind on her sails the greater the righting moments of her keel become and the more efficiently she begins to sail. Apart from the reassurance this stability gives for those with a young family, the boat also has a certain amount of shelter. It is partially decked and being reasonably high-sided, keeps the crew far drier than they would be in a dinghy. The Squib, and others of her size, represent the upward limit of boats that you can trail behind a car and which can be launched and recovered in a few feet of water by members of the family.

The advantages of a boat like this are many: you can choose a different place to sail each time; you haven't the worries of finding a mooring; you haven't the bother of driving down to the coast to see if the boat is still safe after the weather has been stormy and you have the facility of being able to bring the boat home to work on and for winter storage.

But one step up from a boat the size of the Squib and you kiss these benefits good-bye. From now on your boating will become more expensive. You will need a mooring.

The Squib. A natural step-up from a dinghy bringing the family man owner the confident knowledge that with half the entire weight of the boat concentrated below the water in its keel, it will never turn over. Over 500 of these small glass fibre keel boats have been sold.

In all popular boating areas moorings are at a premium and though it may sound rather like putting the cart before the horse, it would be prudent to secure your mooring before choosing your boat. Because the kind of mooring you will get will influence your selection.

It might, for example, decide whether you have a shoal draught boat or a deep keeler.

A shoal draught boat is, as the name implies, one which can float in shallow water. But more than this it has the facility of taking the ground quite comfortably which gives you a far wider choice when seeking a mooring. Probably as many as half the existing free-swinging moorings (where you secure to

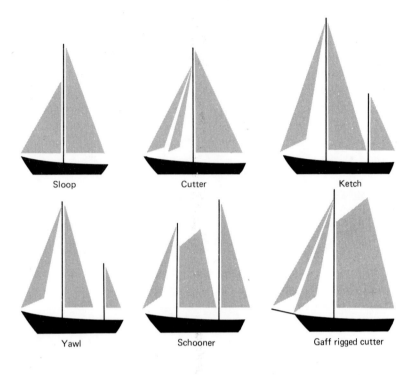

Sloop

Cutter

Ketch

Yawl

Schooner

Gaff rigged cutter

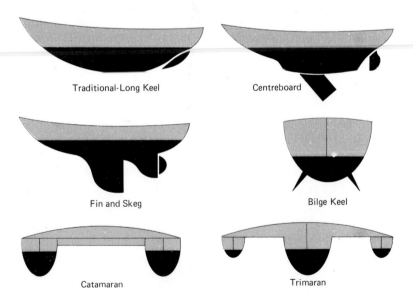

Traditional-Long Keel

Centreboard

Fin and Skeg

Bilge Keel

Catamaran

Trimaran

Fig 5 **Rigs and hull types (silhouettes)**

a buoy) available, are ranged in shallow water where, if they don't dry out at least twice a day at low water, they certainly dry out once a fortnight (at spring tides).

Such half-tide moorings are unsatisfactory for deep keel boats which will lay virtually flat on their sides and possibly even fill with water on the incoming tide. The flat-bottomed, twin keel or centreboard boat is, however, perfectly happy to dry out providing the mooring is reasonably sheltered. It is a wise precaution to check first with the builder to see whether he believes his boat to be adequately constructed to take the ground so frequently. Also check the mooring, chat with other owners and see which boats do take the ground most contentedly. Half-tide moorings are usually cheaper than deep water ones and more often than not are more sheltered and closer to the shore which eliminates the journey in the boat's dinghy (though naturally restricts sailing time).

If you are lucky enough to belong to a yacht club which has deep water moorings, or have climbed to the top of a harbour authority's waiting list, or have chosen the many advantages and extra cost of a marina mooring, then naturally your choice of boat is not so restricted. You could buy a deep keeler. There is no more controversial subject than the comparative merit of shoal draught boats and deep keelers. However, it is accepted – grudgingly by some – that deep keel boats do have the edge on the twin keel boats for windward performance. But in the family cruiser range there is virtually nothing in it and a 24 ft family cruiser with bilge keels will perform practically as well as one with a deep keel. What's more, the bilge keel boat will not only sit upright when it goes aground but will, by its reduced draught be able to go to many places – the heads of rivers and shallow creeks for example – where no deep keel boat would ever dare show her face. On the other hand the bilge keel boat will be able to go anywhere a deep keel boat can go. But let the locality in which you sail and the kind of sailing you wish to do decide for you. If you plan to sail the creeks and rivers and shallow waters then choose a twin keel boat. Alternatively if you want to take part in offshore racing with the Junior Offshore Group or if you habitually keep your boat in deep water then the deep keel boat is the favoured choice.

Bilge keeler dried out happily.

A great deal is talked about the aspect of seaworthiness, and the beginner, especially one who has come straight to a larger boat rather than having begun with a dinghy, may wonder whether the boat he intends buying will be seaworthy. He may feel for example, if he has read of the heroic exploits of some of our contemporary yachtsmen and how they 'rounded the Horn', that anything less than a boat the size of *Gipsy Moth* or *British Steel* and correspondingly equipped is nothing but a deathtrap.

Well let's make it clear straight away that almost without exception every sailing boat built in this country today is seaworthy. And as proof of that we have seen ordinary, small production boats of all types make long ocean passages. The boat you buy *will* be seaworthy and will only cease to be so through your own inexperience or foolishness. Boats are built and designed to withstand some pretty violent conditions but obviously if you plan to sail, shall we say, a small family

A Tomahawk cruiser ready for home completion. This method generally saves the owner between 15 and 20 per cent of the total costs.

cruiser across the Atlantic, which is really taking it away from the sailing it was intended for, and moreover for an extended period, then you will need to make certain changes and modifications. The hull would need strengthening; the rigging would have to be a larger size and the windows reinforced or blanked off etc. These are sensible precautions without which the boat may founder, and yet they do not in themselves suggest that the boat is inherently unseaworthy.

But similarly the boat would *become* unseaworthy if she were overloaded, or if her gear were worn and neglected. And if you were to undertake a passage for which she was obviously not suited – a Mirror to the Mediterranean – or with a crew small in number, inexperienced or weakened by seasickness – then the boat would again be unseaworthy. So you see it all depends upon you.

25

Now after that scripture let's talk more specifically about choosing a boat for the sailing that you plan to do. If you intend to spend the week or weekend aboard a boat, then unless you are prepared to accept the great deal of discomfort and the frustration that accompanies it, you will need a boat of moderate size. Remember that quite apart from the boat's own gear, the sails, tools, navigation instruments, fuel cans, water beakers . . . and the food! each person will need to bring aboard their personal gear, which will invariably include change of clothing, sleeping bag, oilskins, boots, shoes, transistor radio, camera and if you have children – a whole host of products besides, ranging from nappy liners to teddy bears. If any advice can be offered on this score it is to go for the biggest boat you can comfortably afford. Designers may be able to fit four berths on 16 ft water-line length, but that is no recommendation of comfort or even practicality when it comes to spending a week aboard.

Besides, the smaller the boat the more awkward the stowage becomes where so often lockers have to be placed in inaccessible places and even the smallest chore is a major contortion and twice as difficult and tiring. As a guide, if the builder's brochure describes the boat as a five-berther, you can generally reckon that four aboard is the maximum. And don't take too much notice of brochures that show six people in evening dress around the saloon table of a 23 footer boat – they're cardboard cut-outs!

One boat which does give a great deal of comfort in terms of both spaciousness and stability, and without going to great length or tremendous expense is the multihull. And because of its high sail area to displacement ratio and easily driven hulls, it is a very fast boat and exciting to sail. The extra beam which this configuration affords means a large and safe cockpit for children, an enormous deck space for sunbathing and fishing, and a choice of roomy accommodation down below. It is remarkably stable and rolling is kept to a minimum. Indeed it possesses a quality quite unique in sailing – it sails upright! Against these advantages however must be measured its one drawback. Although it is initially very stable it can capsize under certain wild conditions, and if it does capsize, well then that is virtually the end of it. Other minor disadvantages are a certain lack of manoeuvrability in sailing and mooring require-ments and the nasty habit that some harbour authorities have of doubling the multihull's berthing fees.

4 BUYING SECOND-HAND

For most of us the first boat we own will be second-hand. This is not an apology, boats are not like the majority of consumer products where newness is important. Boats are individual. It doesn't matter that they may be old, a little frayed at the edges or have had a string of owners, in fact that may make them more desirable – particularly if they are notable owners! They are not chattels, we don't parade them and it wouldn't impress the sea very much if we did. It doesn't seem to show any more respect for the neighbourhood's newest item of ostentation than a paint-peeling relic of the last century. All it cares about is that the boat should be sound and seaworthy, and there is an abundance of sound and seaworthy boats in the second-hand market.

It must be music to the ears of a poor man to learn that there are definite advantages in buying a boat second-hand – and advantages that you don't get with a new one! To begin with she will have got past her teething troubles. Every boat has them: engines stiff to turn, rudders that squeak, blocks that jam, locks that don't and fastenings that unfasten on their own. But our boat's former owner – who was as conscientious with his upkeep as we are careful in choosing – sorted all these problems out. And moreover he improved the boat in many ways. Perhaps he beefed up the rigging or fitted a more powerful engine, bought some extra winches, fitted up electric lighting or had his wife make bunk cushions and curtains. It is practically certain that if the man cares anything for his boat at all (and some attachments grow as near love as makes no difference) then he will have lavished time and money on her.

Closely allied to these hoped-for improvements is the boat's inventory which, like the improvements, is another thing he must reluctantly let go. For by custom second-hand boats are sold with a complete inventory and you should just turn and walk away from one that is not. By contrast a new boat almost never has a full inventory and this is something that the owner must supplement. In money terms this could be anything from £200 to £2000 and yet when the boat changes hands this becomes included in the price of the boat. This is not to suggest of course that the man who has generously equipped his boat isn't going to ask more than one that hasn't, but even so he will be unlikely to regain anything like the original cost. So it makes sense, when deciding between two otherwise identical boats, to see which offers the more extras. And then again if you are particularly lucky the sale of a second-hand boat may include ownership or right of a mooring as well.

But these are the hidden benefits and some of them may be so well hidden as not to be visible at all. The main advantage in buying second-hand is that you get more boat for your money! Or in other words you could, due to normal depreciation and the fact that you are not liable to pay VAT, buy a larger boat than you might otherwise be able to afford.

Not that everyone wants or can afford the upkeep of a large boat, but as size is something to be equated with comfort, windward performance, liveability, cruising range, safety and speed, a bigger boat is what people generally aim for. In yachting's more splendid days they used to say that the length of your boat should be one foot for each year of your age. That might have been a good yardstick for the social aspirant of the 1920s but it hardly makes sense today, besides it puts an awful heavy strain on the old age pensioners.

The first time buyer is ill advised to buy a very large boat. They demand a great deal more experience. In a little boat you can easily push yourself off when you go aground or fend-off with your hand when an erratic course seems to threaten the future of the pier. But in bigger boats there are bigger forces and any damage is likely to be costlier and more extensive. The beginner with a big boat is as dangerous to himself and others as the Sunday driver who gets behind the wheel of a juggernaut. He should start small, learn the job and just keep the big boat on his horizon.

The old boat has never aspired to that happy state that the old motor car enjoys – veteran value. There are hundreds of boats sixty or seventy years old still sailing, and still selling

Veteran boats are still in great demand and there is a strong sense of comradeship amongst their owners. This one has put up everything she has got to race with the Solent 'Old Gaffers'.

quite cheaply. They are of course admired. We praise their endurance, their character and construction but few of us ever seem to want to own them – at least not to a degree that they are ever in such great demand. Consequently they remain cheap, and for the man with time and enthusiasm to maintain them, they can be a very good buy.

Still it must be borne in mind that boats of this vintage *do* demand a great deal more attention than modern boats. What's more they are slower and generally poor performers to windward; they are – length for length – less roomy inside, their gear is heavier and, unless you are able to do the work yourself, they can be very expensive to maintain. There is no reason at all why an old boat need not be sound, but with age against her you may have difficulty in (a) raising a loan to buy her and (b) getting her insured. Against this, you will find that boats in maturity have a charm and fascination that you'll never find in a glass fibre creation. Wives beware! They are perfectly capable of breaking up homes and marriages.

Unless entirely bewitched or determined the newcomer should resist the temptation to buy an old boat; they, like the big ones, require more skill in handling. Far better to buy a young stripling – one of the many small family cruisers that make up the nucleus of the second-hand market.

SEARCHING FOR A BOAT

There is no ideal boat any more than there is an ideal wife; they are all a compromise of sorts, it's just that some suit you better than others. And you will in all probability grow to love them, faults and favours alike. You simply have to make sure that they'll be well endowed with the latter and not too many faults.

Search thoroughly but don't go to enormous distances. There really is no need. Some people spend a small fortune in fuel and fares scouring the country for their ideal boat when in fact a search in their own boating locality would be almost certain to reveal a boat that would perfectly well suit them. And this isn't just a case of the globe-trotting Romeo who finally marries the girl next door, it is simply a case of logic. In any one of our popular yachting centres there are thousands upon thousands of boats to choose from, thousands of girls-next-door. Besides if you were to find your 'ideal' tucked away in the Outer Hebrides then apart from travelling expenses and phone calls you will have the frightening expense of bringing her home. These will outweigh all the advantages of buying in a 'low-price area'.

Once you have determined the type of boat you want then be as specific as your pocket will allow and visit all the local boatyards and brokers. If they haven't got what you want then you can leave your requirements with them and you'll be surprised just how quickly something will turn up! Remember too that *any* boat is for sale at the right price and if you see one that takes your fancy it may well be worth contacting the owner – it just could be the inheritance of a penniless widow who hates boats and anything to do with sailing.

It is almost certain that you will be spending a great deal of time scanning the small ad pages of yachting magazines and provincial newspapers. Boats can seem so much more attractive when anchored to your office desk, on the platform of the railway station or on the canteen table at lunchtime. Be patient, don't journey miles to see a boat without first writing to ask the owner for specific details. 'Aux Bm CB sloop, LOA 35 ft Lloyds 100A1, RT, DF, E/S etc.' isn't much of a description to go by, even when you've conquered the abbreviations. Ask the man to send you some photographs which he should be prepared to do if he realizes you have a long distance to travel.

There may be no such thing as an ideal boat but there is an ideal time to buy one. It is early autumn when the present owner has just had his season's fun and now faces the expense of laying her up and storing her for the winter. He will also have a great many jobs and repairs to be done. It is a good time to buy also because it will give the buyer plenty of time to get her ready for next season. The very worst time to buy (and likewise best time to sell) is the first sunny day of spring when the trees are in blossom, the birds are in song and there is sunlight dancing on the water! Good time to unload leaky old sports cars too, they tell me!

Finally, remember that the quoted price is the amount the buyer *hopes* to get, he expects you to offer less. Turn away from the ad that says 'no offers' – you won't like the man anyway. Look for the one that is suffixed 'o.n.o.' and go in with the boot.

THE SURVEY

Always have a second-hand boat surveyed no matter who you are buying it from or whatever the recommendation. It may be that even with the best and most honest intentions the seller is unaware of faults the boat has. It is practically impossible for an amateur to conduct a proper survey; to tell, for example, whether the boat has been strained or weakened, whether the keel bolts are sound, whether the underwater fittings have been weakened with electrolytic action, or whether the timber in vital but unseen places has fallen victim to rot or the notorious gribble worm. Only an experienced surveyor will be able to determine the existence of such things. A survey of course costs money and it costs more money if the boat is in the water and has to be slipped, or have part of its interior furniture removed or its keel bolts drawn. However, it is an investment because if the boat turns out to have a serious defect then it will have saved you a great deal of money in having to pay for it to be put right. Besides there is always the chance that if smaller defects are found the present owner will have to drop the price or agree to contribute to the repair cost. Place a deposit on a boat by all means, but always ensure that this is paid 'subject to survey'.

A survey should indicate two kinds of defects – if any exist at all that is. Those which must be put right before the boat may be considered to be in a seaworthy condition, and secondly those faults which, while they might not affect the boat's safety and performance, *will* have to be put right eventually. You can judge then from these, and the surveyor's summing up at the end, whether the boat is still a good buy and how much it will cost to put the faults to right. You may also be able to ask the surveyor to comment on the price being asked for the boat, although don't be disappointed if his answer is not absolutely direct.

Surveyors advertise in yachting magazines or you may be able to get your insurance company to recommend one. Failing this you could write to the Yacht Brokers, Designers and Surveyors Association who will supply a list of surveyors who may be relied upon to do a good job. Lloyds Register of Shipping also carry out yacht surveys. In choosing a surveyor try to pick one who lives near the locality of the boat because you will have to pay for his travelling expenses and his lunch. If you have selected two or three boats in the same area then it may be worthwhile asking the surveyor to inspect all three first, as a sort of package deal, and let you know which he considers to be the best of the lot, before going ahead with a proper survey. And, incidentally, an inspection by a surveyor can be an inexpensive measure of deciding whether a survey is worthwhile or not!

If you cannot get hold of a surveyor, then a qualified boat-builder would be a good substitute. In any event don't go to the offices of a local fishing type or the waterfront bum that you meet in the pub. Their expertise is rarely up to the standard of their stories.

THE BUSINESS OF PURCHASE

Ask the seller to make two lists of the inventory he plans to let go with the boat, then there will be no argument later when he insists that he never intended the mast and sails should go in with the price. If the boat is registered (which means she is registered as a 'British Ship', has an official number assigned by the Department of Trade, has registration papers and her official number carved into her beam) then you will need a Bill of Sale to augment the transaction. This is available from the HM Stationery Office. You will also need a Declaration of Ownership form and both will have to be completed. Upon receipt of the purchase money the owner signs the Bill of Sale and has it witnessed. This in itself is a full receipt and stipulates that the vessel is sold free from encumbrances. The owner then sends these documents and the ship's papers to HM Customs office at the vessel's port of registry where the new owner's name is recorded and note made that he is now the owner.

It is very difficult, when buying an unregistered boat, to safeguard yourself against the possibility of an undischarged hire purchase debt or any other bill that the previous owner has left unpaid. For the responsibility is automatically transferred to you! There is no collective pool of information about hire purchase debts as there is in the motor trade. However, the Bill of Sale does contain a clause to the effect that the yacht and its many parts are free from incumbrances and you should also see that the previous owner signs a declaration that the boat is sold 'entirely free from all debts and claims whatsoever'.

5 BUILDING YOUR OWN CRUISER

You no longer have to be a time-served shipwright to build your own boat, the skills of the average kitchen-chair carpenter will suffice. In some cases you'll manage with less than that; just so long as you've the gumption to read the directions, follow the parts and have done a few jig-saw puzzles at some time in your life.

Marine plywood, glass fibre, resin glue, barbed nails, epoxy preparations, rubber sealing compounds, fibre-glass sheathing, metal mast extusion, pop rivets, Perspex . . . these are just a few of the hundreds of products and materials that have made it all possible, that have brought about the boat-building revolution. These items and a breed of far seeing designers have swept away the covers that kept yachting in the hands of a few and now it's for anyone who wants to enjoy it. If you want to own a boat, build one! Determination is the main requirement.

Let's talk about this special requirement. How much determination do you have? Because there is probably a home-built boat that will suit your special capacity. Do you have the kind of determination to hand your fireside chair over to the cat on a cold frosty night and work by the light of a candle at the bottom of the garden . . . and do that perhaps for two or three years? If not, you shouldn't consider building a boat from scratch. Do you then have lots of determination, but lots of children also and an equally determined wife? In which case you hadn't better start from first base either. Your boat will grow just high enough to haunt you and only come into prominence when a row on family expenses flares up. Better to settle on something smaller or buy the part-completed boat where you have only to add a few fittings. Finally, if yours is the fiery kind of determination that burns fiercely for a few months and then fizzles out altogether, then you really shouldn't start at all because boatbuilding doesn't like that kind of builder.

Closely linked to determination is time. It takes a profes-

sional about six months to build a moderate sized cruiser –
that's a wooden boat starting from the keel. Now of course he
is a skilled man who fully understands the sequence of the job,
he is working in ideal conditions with plenty of room and light
and he has all the right tools to hand. Spread the number of
hours this entails into weekends, holidays and a few summer
evenings and put them in the hands of an amateur who must
stop at frequent intervals to pore over the plans and it can add
up to at least three years! A 24 ft plywood cruiser fully rigged
and fitted out takes a good 1500 hours.

So how much time does your job or family or social life
allow? Would it be expedient to spend more hours at work
in order to earn more money and pay for a part built boat?
This is a more productive arrangement and although it does
rather ignore the pleasure and relaxation that can be got from
hours with a hammer and saw it is still a worthwhile consideration. In this case the kit-built boat might suit you, where for
example the glass fibre hull and deck are supplied together
with all fittings including mast, sails and engine, and with every
wooden part numbered and cut to size. A 24 ft cruiser of
this type can usually be completed in 300 hours – although
naturally the saving is smaller.

The important thing is not to take on more than you can
successfully hope to accomplish, and this particularly applies
with the question of money. A delusion which many of us
suffer from is believing that when we build or buy the bare
hull of a boat that there is little more to do. Perhaps because it
represents the greater part of the boat's entire shape. we tend
to think of it in exaggerated terms. But in fact the hull represents
only one-third of the boat's overall cost and only one-third
of its building time. When considering whether to build or
buy a hull there may not seem to be much difference in costs
between say, a thirty footer and a forty footer. But remember
for a true evaluation that difference must be multiplied three
times!

Remember this and bear it in mind but on the other hand
don't allow it to influence you to build a boat smaller than you
really need. There is no greater disappointment than to labour
long and hard over a boat only to find she is too small, cramped
and a poor performer.

Amazing what some enthusiasts can hatch in their back gardens.

Another consideration is a place to build your boat. You may be able to rent a space at a boatyard which is useful inasmuch as you will have chandlery close to hand, power probably, the saved expense of having to get the completed boat to the water and the facility of professional advice. You will also get a lot of unprofessional advice from other builders in the yard. Nevertheless it can be handy and someone is bound to know where you can get cheap fittings or where there is a good run of pitch going for the asking. And incidentally, this brings us to a very important point in home building which is to tell everyone what you are doing. It is amazing the undiscovered skills that friends can possess, quite apart from an uncanny knack they may have of finding 'things'.

The drawback of renting boatyard space is the cost and the fact that you may have a long way to journey. This means time lost and extra cost for not only have you the expense of travelling, and you'll need the car to carry the tools, but it also precludes putting in the odd hour or two that you could easily manage if the boat were in the back garden. Another point about boatyard building is that you're always forgetting to bring down the right tools with you.

The ideal place to build is in your back garden under cover. The importance of cover cannot be stressed too much. It need only be a frame and polythene shelter but the time spent in its construction will be amply rewarded in hours saved in rainy day working, in better glued joints, dry timber and comfort, for at least under cover you can arrange some kind of heating. One grave warning, however, if you are confronted with any kind of access, be it the space between houses or gateposts, be absolutely certain of your measurements before starting. If that magnificent engineer Isambard Kingdom Brunel could build the *Great Britain* six inches wider than the width of the dock gates, then the same thing can happen to you! And if building really big then find out from the council what new developments are going on around you. One man recently built a 70 ft ferro-cement boat in a field only to find that a housing estate had sprung up around him.

THE PARTLY COMPLETED BOAT

Apart from those firms which specialize in kit boats where all the parts come complete in a packing case, there are many other builders who will build you a boat to different stages of completion. (In fact you could probably get any builder of glass fibre boats to do so enabling you a very wide choice. But unless they usually trade this way, they would probably be reluctant or unwilling to have you keep popping back to ask questions and take measurements etc.) Exactly what stage of completion you desire depends on the things we discussed formerly, but perhaps the most advantageous stage – that is to say to make the biggest saving while avoiding most of the

37

difficult work – is to have hull and deck bonded together with bulkheads, floors, engine bearers all fitted; and perhaps even the engine fitted, because this too is a skilled operation.

This stage leaves you all the interior furniture to complete and allows you a layout of your own choice (within limits). It also allows you to pay for the boat as the work progresses, and buy the parts as and when you can afford them. Perhaps even pick up second-hand items. It is difficult to state exactly how much this method saves but it is usually between 15 and 20 per cent of the completed boat. This may sound miserably little and far less than you hoped or the advertisements implied. But then as any handyman knows it is practically impossible to compete in price with items of mass or batch production. Apart from buying his materials in bulk and therefore more cheaply, the big operator is properly geared up to the work. He has jigs and formers and a workforce that is familiar with the problems that you in your cramped little shed will spend hours puzzling over. Nor will he make the mistakes or waste the material that you do. Virtually all you save is labour time which costs you nothing. And your own labour is the only thing which you will not have to pay VAT on, by the way, for even part built boats are subject to this tax.

Estimates on the number of hours needed to complete a boat from hull and deck stage vary. Some will work flat out for a quick result while others will work painstakingly and not be content until every detail is absolutely correct. But as a general rule it is considered that 600 hours should complete a 24 ft cruiser.

STARTING FROM THE KEEL

Building a boat from scratch gives you a freedom of choice not possible with the other methods. You can have virtually any design of boat you wish in virtually any material. But let's take it from the standpoint of the first time builder who perhaps hasn't the confidence to build a tops'l schooner in pre-stressed cabbage stalks or whatever the next revolutionary material may be. He will almost certainly need not only a set of plans from a notable designer but also a set of working drawings and instructions to follow. It will be helpful too if he knows that

38

there are others who have gone before him so that he could possibly correspond or go and see them. As for the material he can choose, this will depend on its price, availability, ease with which it can be worked and, most important of all, how happy the builder feels with it. For example, it may be that ferro-cement is the most economical method of home construction but if you feel more at home with wood and dislike concrete and steel, then it is obviously not your material.

The three most popular materials for the amateur are foam sandwich, ferro-cement and plywood. There are others such as cold moulding with thin veneers of wood, steel and one which incorporates the use of glass fibre 'planking'. There are even more simplified methods of wood building, such as strip planking, but we'll confine our remarks to those which are more popular.

Marine Plywood

There are many designs for plywood boats together with full working drawings and even associations like the Eventide Owners Club who can offer help to builders considering building to this class. Construction is comparatively simple in that curves are in one plane only and the shell is built on sawn or fabricated frames – no complicated bending involved. It is a slower method of building than ferro-cement or foam sandwich but probably falls midway between the two in cost. Time is saved in fitting out the interior because the furniture is easier to fit to the wooden hull.

Ferro-Cement

This requires the minimum amount of skill and the crudest of materials – water pipe, chicken wire, sand and cement. It consists of a steel framework covered with wire and plastered with mortar. It is in reality a steel boat encased with mortar. To date it is easily the cheapest form of home construction and has the added advantage that the hull, at least, can be built without any form of cover. However, the plastering, which would be done in one day by a team of hired professionals, must be done between spring and autumn when there are no frosts in the air.

39

The hull of a 40 ft ferro-cement **boat** being launched.

A ferro-hull can be built very quickly in a matter of three or four months but thereafter the fitting out takes as long as any other boat. It is normal to fit a wooden deck. The finish that it is possible to get with a ferro-cement hull can range from perfection to bloomin' awful and for the builder's own satisfaction, quite apart from re-sale value, he would be advised to buy a stock design with the frames already bent to shape, the wire mesh, the properly selected sand and cement and the specially prepared epoxy-fillers and paints all supplied. Moreover this arrangement usually affords him the advice of an expert who can assist him and take charge on the nail-biting occasion of plastering day when everything must run to a proper schedule. He will also be able to arrange the employment of plasterers. This arrangement will add considerably to the cost but having seen so many ferro-boats where the builder laboured alone with only the crude materials, believe me it is money well spent.

Foam Sandwich

This too is a relatively quick way to build a hull although it costs more than the other two methods. The shape of the boat is first constructed crudely in something like demolition timber. Next, sections of specially prepared foam are laid over the frame and temporarily fastened to it. The foam in turn is covered with several layers of glass fibre cloth, matting and resin to form the outside skin. It is finished with a filler coat which is rubbed down to give it an attractive and durable surface. The boat is then turned over, the wood framing removed and layers of glass fibre cloth or mat are bonded to the inside of the foam.

Alternatives

A few years ago a young man called John Ridler caught the imagination of many when he built a boat of his own and sailed her twice across the Atlantic. His boat, which was called *Eric the Red*, cost £165! The boat's seaworthiness was proved beyond doubt but it is doubtful whether she would have lasted for many years. Nonetheless it does show that it is still possible to build a boat cheaply, even at today's extortionate prices. And just as a way of incentive let's look at some other savings.

John Ridler made his own sails and there is certainly no objection to doing this. Sailmaking is not difficult, it's a fraction of the cost. Alternatively, you can pick up second-hand sails and have them altered.

Lead has always been considered the only sensible ballast but there are thousands of yachts today sailing quite safely with lumps of iron in their keels – sash weights are a special favourite, although it is important to fix them securely, otherwise, when the boat heels excessively, they are likely to rain down on you.

Timber is one of the most expensive items but with the amount of demolition that has gone on in recent years it is not difficult to pick up suitable lengths of pitch pine and oak at knock-down prices. Similarly, interior furniture can be made with the less conventional tongue and groove 'knotty pine' or from parts of old furniture sold off at auctions.

A marine engine is also expensive but perfectly good diesel engines can be bought from vehicle scrapyards, particularly if the vehicle was 'written-off' through being involved in an accident, and there are many firms which specialize in supplying the parts to 'marinize' a commercial engine.

The list of ideas is endless: telegraph pole masts, telegraph pole rigging screws, drums of paint 'slops' from paint manufacturers, Sandtex for deck paints, waterpipe guardrails, plastic toilet bends for ventilators, scaffold pipes for spars . . . nothing around the house will be safe once you get started.

6 BUYING NEW

So far we have talked about how to decide on a choice of boat and how your own circumstances, rather than your enthusiasm, should really dictate the choice. How your finances, your fitness and capability, the amount of spare time you have, the size and spacing of your children and the locality and passages you hope you can make . . . how these things have taken hold of your dream boat and put it into a work-a-day shape.

We have talked too about the many aspects of home building and how again, in contrast to what the poets say, your grasp shouldn't exceed your reach. We have explored the second-hand market and found a few pitfalls. Now it is time to look at the new boats and the things to consider when purchasing new.

Unlike the car industry, which has contracted into a handful of major companies, there are literally hundreds of boatbuilding companies. There are big firms and small firms and no guideline to say which produces the best quality – the firm with the multi-national connections or the yard where everyone sleeps under the bench. Both are as capable of building something lovely as they are of building a lemon – it's up to the buyer to discover who builds which.

But in case this implies that buying a new boat is as chancy as doing the weekly shop in an Arab bazaar, then let me quickly assure you that it is not. It is true that you do have to go into the market place for your intelligence but it presents no problem. The boat world is a close-knit society and you would only need to let the word drop in the yacht club, along the waterfront or wherever boat people gather, that you planned to buy such-and-such a boat and their reactions will tell you all you need to know. The unguarded smile, the eyes that roll heavenwards, the startled gasp – these things are hard for people who love boats to cover up, although they are usually very much more vociferous! It really takes no time at all to learn who builds the best boats, it's as good as a *Which?* market survey.

So far as customer safeguards are concerned these are not nearly so clearly defined as they are in, say, the motor car industry. Some builders do offer a one-year guarantee against material failure or faulty workmanship but these are in the minority. Most builders however belong to the Ship and Boatbuilders National Federation and apart from laying down terms of trading they will investigate complaints with reasonable thoroughness. In fact you would be unwise to deal with a boat firm that was not a member.

Another thing to look for is the Lloyds mouldings certificates. Some builders tend to over-play this as if to imply that the entire boat is built to the requirements of this august and unremitting body. Certainly a boat can be built 'under Lloyds' where every nut and bolt used would have to conform to required type and size and there would be periodic inspections by a Lloyds surveyor, but for the ordinary standard glass fibre boat a 'series moulding certificate' is more usually awarded. This means that the glass fibre mouldings have been constructed to Lloyds' recommendation and that the conditions in the factory where they have been moulded have been found satisfactory, i.e. they are not being made under damp and humid conditions. But there you are; the parts may be in perfect condition although there is nothing to say that they haven't been put together by a monkey.

But, in all, complaints of bad workmanship or material fault are few and this is probably because the boat industry has remained small and competitive. You can still collar the man who built your boat and tell him what you think of him. He's not hidden behind a wall of agents, distributors, personal aides and brute-faced secretaries. He is available, and assailable, and if you think you have had a raw deal you can easily march in and tell him. Nine out of ten times the matter can be sorted out; imagine, in contrast trying to get Henry Ford on the phone to tell him your Cortina's exhaust has just fallen off!

A guide to what might be the most suitable make of boat for the area in which you intend to sail are the numbers of them that are there already. A preponderance of one type may be the result of local fashion and fancy but it is likely to be attributed to good sound reasons such as the fact that the boat has been specifically designed for the conditions of the area. Or, less subtly, the builder's yard might be handy and you haven't to worry about delivery charges.

For those who are not able to ferret around for this kind of information there is always the chance to see what the industry has to offer at the ever growing number of boat shows. Only rarely does the boat industry enthuse itself sufficiently to go out and grab customers, but at boat shows it does so quite successfully. And you stand a very good chance of seeing your pre-conceived notions of size, price and type evaporate at the sight of a mermaid's cleavage and the cork coming out of a bottle. Use the boat show basically for what it is – a chance to compare one boat with another. Remember too that a boat will look wholly different and disappointingly smaller in the water. Choose your boat and place a deposit if you must do, after the confirmation of a firm delivery date, but do insist on a sail demonstration before purchase.

There are some builders who now ask for a deposit before a demonstration. Happily these are few, and most builders, if they believe you to be genuinely interested, will be glad to give you a free demonstration. And why not indeed when you consider what other salesmen would give to have a 'captive' audience for a few hours. Besides, most builders are only too happy to put their new boat through its paces. They are honestly proud of their creations and that, by the way, is a mark of the industry!

INVENTORY – IS THE BOAT 'READY FOR SEA'?

It is impossible to make an accurate comparison between the listed price of one boat and another without taking into account the many items of gear which one builder may have included and another omitted. One builder may perhaps have kitted his boat out with everything you could possibly need down to knife, fork and spoon while the other may not even list an anchor – although this is a little extreme. Nevertheless, there are many shades in between and it is an incautious buyer who does not check exactly what is included in the 'standard price'. Though I must hasten to add that it isn't necessarily a deception on the builder's part to leave important items out of the inventory and therefore the price. He may, for example, decide that the very cheapest type of compass (which the other builder has quoted and included in his price) is not at all suitable or even reliable for his customers.

Check how many items are included in the builder's standard inventory and how near the boat then comes to his claim that she is ready for sea! (See chapter 7.)

REGISTRATION

It is not essential that a small boat under 15 tons net tonnage should be registered as a British ship, which means that it will have an official number, assigned through the Department of Trade and Industry and be issued with registration papers in a similar fashion to a car, but nonetheless it is an advantage. To begin with it is a proof of ownership and it will certainly save a great deal of explanations with foreign port officials should you decide to cruise in other countries – in fact it is almost imperative that your boat be registered if you are to go abroad. Finally if you propose to buy the boat on a marine mortgage, rather than through a hire purchase agreement, then registration of the craft is necessary. This applies specifically to larger boats; dinghies are not usually registered.

MORTGAGE OR HIRE PURCHASE

A marine mortgage is available only to registered boats and it works in the same way as a house mortgage, where the property legally belongs to the owner all the time and the mortgagee is merely lending him the money for purchase at an agreed rate of interest. It has the other advantage that the repayment period is generally longer than that of hire purchase agreements and that the interest paid can be off-set against income tax. It is worth 'shopping around' for the most favourable terms.

INSURANCE

There is no legal requirement to insure a boat but it is a sensible precaution; not only to cover the cost of possible damage, replacing after theft etc., but also to cover for third party claims and passenger risks. Personal accidents and injury are not uncommon in the rough and tumble life afloat and it could very easily be that somebody may slap in a claim against you. Generally insurance cover is confined to six months in the water and six months out, although this can be extended so that you could sail later than October or earlier than April or indeed any weekend between. However, you will have to notify your insurance company. A telephone call is usually sufficient. Study your insurance cover. It may not cover you to sail single-handed nor even to foreign parts without an additional premium. Similarly, you may need extra cover if you plan to race your boat. Be honest and fair about this, marine insurance companies are generally very good in settling justifiable claims promptly and in full. But if you try to claim for ice damage when your boat was only covered for a summer in the Solent, well then you may not get a penny.

DEPRECIATION

Boats tend to hold their prices very well and in these days of inflation they may well appreciate in value. However, like most investments one has to choose sensibly, nothing of mere fashion, nothing too outrageous in design. While of course it finally depends on how well the boat is maintained.

7 BARE-BONE NECESSITIES

It is not possible to itemize every single piece of equipment that you'll need for the boat in just this one chapter. The new cruising boatman, stocking what is virtually a second home and workshop as well, will have started his collection long ago – *Cutty Sark* tea towel; three cork life-jackets; sixteen cups without handles; his shopping list is endless.

Nor, within these pages do we want to get involved in the interminable argument about gadgets – whether an Inertial Navigation System is necessary for a cross-Channel trip or is a Mickey Mouse compass good enough? All we really want to do is to list those essential items that you will have to provide before you can set safely to sea in your boat.

Every boat, no matter how small, must have the following:

An Anchor

With a rope or chain attached permanently to it. An anchor is your break, your holdfast. If your oar breaks; your mast carries away; your sails tear, your engine fails or your skipper jumps over the side (which in the wake of that lot is likely!), then the anchor is the only way by which you can stop the boat being blown out to sea/washed on the rocks/swept over the weir/smacked into the harbour wall/ and so on. . . .

A Bailer

Or some means of rapidly discharging water in the event of the boat being swamped. Even racing dinghies fitted with self-bailing systems need to carry a bailer because the former only functions when the boat is moving. In larger boats the bailer usually gives way to a bilge pump, although it has been said that no pump can match the speed and capacity of a frightened yachtsman with a bucket.

A Compass

You have to experience the feeling of absolute disorientation that the descent of a fog can bring to a boat before you really appreciate the need for a compass. The shoreline evaporates, the horizon does too and with only the small patch of sea that surrounds you visible, you lose all sense of direction; you might be heading safely for the harbour entrance or you might be off to America – only a compass can tell you.

Distress Signals

These are available in a kit and come in a waterproof packet. They usually contain hand-held flares which give off a bright red light plus a number of orange-coloured smoke flares for use in the daytime. Larger boats should also include in their kit a number of rockets which show red stars. Unhappily today the small boatman is in as much danger from being run down by a ship as he is from exposure to the natural elements. For this reason it is wise to carry a number of white flares that can be ignited on the near approach of a vessel so as to indicate your existence. Such flares, the diffident will note, do not bring out the emergency services.

A Lifebuoy

If a man falls over the side while the boat is making way it can be very difficult to see or hear him – indeed at night or in rough seas it is practically impossible. So the lifebuoy that you had the presence of mind to throw, or he had the good fortune to take with him, will not only support him but also serve as a marker. And if it is a bright, orange coloured lifebuoy with a self igniting light and whistle attached to it, then so much the better.

One good long Rope

In addition to the usual mooring warps and anchor cable. It will have a multiplicity of uses but serve principally as a tow line – both for you and other people.

49

A Torch

This is not merely my recommendation but an international ruling. Indeed for larger boats there are precise instructions as to the kind and the colour of lights that should be carried (see chapter 11) but for dinghies and all open rowing boats a powerful, waterproof torch is sufficient. It is used to indicate your presence to approaching vessels at night and also to illuminate the compass.

A Means to Determine the Depth of Water

It may either be a boathook marked with white painted rings, a sounding line knotted at intervals and weighted with a lead sinker or an electronic echo sounder.

A Noise-Making Instrument

A strange suggestion but again it is an international ruling. Vessels in fog are required to indicate their position by making sound signals and it is usual for vessels under 40 ft to make their sound, while making way, at intervals of one minute. Hunting horns, whistles, or small aerosol-can sirens can be used, although in larger boats the old box-shaped Norwegian fog horn is the most efficient.

A Chart

In a small dinghy it is often impractical to carry a chart (although they can be folded and kept inside a plastic wallet) in which case the owner should thoroughly familiarize himself with the area and its dangers before setting out. People have been known to sail with road maps, but as these don't yet show such things as submerged rocks, tide rips, lighthouses, telegraph cables and gunnery practice areas they must be considered hopelessly inadequate.

This completes the standard inventory for *all* boats of whatever description or configuration. There are however several additions for particular types of craft.

DINGHIES

Buoyancy Arrangements

Both sailing dinghies and small rowing dinghies used by larger craft as tenders must carry either inflatable air-bags, or have built-in buoyancy chambers to keep them afloat in the event of their being capsized or swamped.

Oars

Sailing dinghies must carry either a set of oars and rowlocks, or a set of paddles should they suffer a dismasting or similar disability.

CRUISING BOATS

Radar Reflector

It was mentioned earlier that the small boat owner's biggest fear, while sailing near shipping lanes, is the chance of being run down. The danger is of course increased at night or in poor visibility when the big ships are navigating by radar. This is because the echo from the hull of a small boat becomes imperceptible from the echoes of the waves which surround her. A radar reflector hoisted high up the mast sharpens the boat's echo on their radar screens. It doesn't guarantee that you will be seen but it very much improves your chances.

A Tender

Even if you could be sure to find a berth alongside in every port you visited there would still be the odd occasion when you would need a dinghy (or a *tender* as it is called in this instance). If you go aground it may be the only way to run out a kedge anchor, or it could turn out to be your lifeboat. Either an inflatable or traditional dinghy can be used, it is a matter of preference.

Every dinghy should carry a set of paddles. One paddle and a part of the broken mast can never propel the boat properly; besides it leads to arguments.

Fire Extinguisher

At least one but preferably more should be carried. Fire and explosion are the biggest single hazard at sea and what makes it so much worse is that if a fire takes hold you are trapped with only the sea for refuge – and that's no refuge at all on a cold and stormy night.

A Kedge – or Second Anchor

This may be used as a back-up for the main anchor or it may be used in crowded waters to prevent the boat swinging around with the tide, but more probably it will be used to help pull the boat off the bottom should you have the misfortune of going aground.

52

Guardrails, Pulpits and Stanchions

These combine to make up the 'railings' which run round the outside of the boat. Although not strictly necessary in very small cruisers where the sails can be handed through the fore-hatch or from the cockpit, they are however essential in a larger boat. Without the handholds they provide all work on deck would be either impossible or very dangerous. They are also essential where children are carried.

First Aid Kit

There is no need to turn the boat into a cottage hospital but the kit should at least contain bandages; cotton wool; disinfectant; sticking plaster; burn dressings; scissors; tweezers; aspirins; suntan lotion and a manual of instruction. Seasick tablets an optional extra.

Fenders and Warps

You will need at least four warps (larger boats may need more), a bow line, stern line and two 'springs'. They should each be about two and a half times the length of the boat.

Heaving Line

A small light line about 12 fathoms long which can be easily thrown and used for passing heavier ropes etc. It will need to have a weighted end to enable it to be thrown.

Tide Tables and Tidal Atlas (see chapter 13)

Transistor Radio

To be used for listening to weather forecasts.

CRUISERS FITTED WITH ENGINES

Tools

And such necessary spares as sparking plugs (spare sheer pin and starting cord for the outboard engine), plug leads, drive belts, etc.

Spare Fuel

On too many occasions lifeboat crews are called out to go to the aid of a boat which has run out of fuel. It is a diabolical crime to use the emergency services in this way and they would be fully justified in claiming salvage! If your fuel is petrol make sure it is carried in a proper container (not plastic) and that it is clearly marked. You should also carry a funnel and spare lubricating oil.

The list of items so far accords very nicely with my conscience; I mean I am happy that you can put to sea in moderate safety without having pawned your belongings, put your wife on the streets or your children into care. It doesn't, of course, allow you a great deal of comfort and if you want to eat, sleep or go to the toilet in a civilized fashion, then you are going to have to spend a great deal more. But that's understood isn't it?

Finally, and particularly if you are going to sea in somebody else's boat you will need: a life-jacket; safety harness; oilskins (many dinghy sailors prefer to wear wet suits); non-slip deck shoes or boots; torch; knife; shackle key; and spare clothing all packed away in a kit bag or soft holdall.

8 HANDLING THE BOAT

If there is one thing which puzzles the newcomer to sailing, it is how – when there is obviously only one wind – do boats all manage to sail in different directions?

He can comprehend that a boat can be blown along by the wind – anything can! He can even see, that given enough momentum, a boat can turn back on itself and begin to go back to where it came from . . . but how does it manage to maintain it? How is it that a boat can sail *into* the wind?

Beating to windward, as this particular point of sailing is called, is mystifying enough to merit an explanation.

To make a boat sail into the wind (and 45 degrees will be about the nearest she can manage) it is first necessary to haul in both the main and jib sheets so that the sails are trimmed more or less down the centre-line of the boat. In this position they look to be flat but if you could view them from the top of the mast you would see that they are aerofoil in shape, similar to the wing of an aircraft. There is a deep curve down the leading edge or *luff* of the sail which gradually flattens away at the leach or after part. This is known as the sail's *camber*.

When the boat is moving forward, the air quite naturally passes on both sides of the sail, but, whereas the air stream that passes along the inside of the curve has a fairly unimpeded passage, the air stream on the outside is not so fortunate; it has the billow of the sail to contend with. In other words it has further to travel, and because it has further to travel so it must also travel faster.

But when the movement of air, or a fluid, is accelerated it becomes 'stretched', or in more precise terms it experiences a drop in pressure. The air pressure on the inside of the sail however remains unaltered and so there becomes a difference in air pressure between one side of the sail and the other. The higher pressure on the inside then forces the sail into the low

55

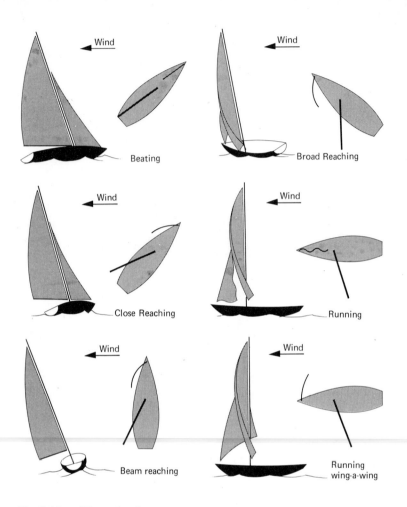

Fig 6 Handling the boat

pressure area and as this is a continuous action so the sail (and the boat) is perpetually driven forward.

In practice only a fraction of the force is driving the boat forward; most of it is trying to push the boat sideways, downwind. In fact if the boat were flat-bottomed with absolutely no underwater projection, then downwind is exactly where she would go. This is known as making *leeway*.

Leeway is counteracted by the yacht's deep underwater shape (a centre plate does the same thing in a dinghy) which offers a large area of lateral resistance to re-direct the force into a forward movement. Bilge keels, leeboards and dagger boards all perform the same function. This is how a boat is made to sail forward into the wind.

The drawing force described is present with each sail and each would be capable of pushing the boat along independently. But there is also an added force from the interaction between the two sails, the mainsail and the jib.

With the jib set slightly ahead and to one side of the mainsail a narrow gap is formed. This is called the *slot*. Air passing through this slot and onto the outside of the mainsail is constricted and, like water squeezing through the nozzle of a garden hose, it is considerably speeded up. Because of this acceleration it suffers a still further drop in pressure which in turn results in an even greater pressure difference between the air on each side of the mainsail. In this way yet more driving force is created.

But if the slot is too wide then the entire effect is lost. While on the other hand, if the slot is too narrow, the air flow contorts and deflects against the outside of the mainsail causing it to shake. The jib is then said to be *backwinding* the main.

This is one of the points to watch when beating to windward although it is just as important to see that the luff of the jib or the mainsail doesn't also begin to shake. When this happens it means the boat is being *pinched*, or sailed too close to the wind and as a result some of the wind is blowing on the inside of the jib. This *lifting* of the luff of the jib is usually accompanied by a drop in speed.

Alternatively, if the boat were to be sailed too far off the wind (too *free*) then the speed would increase but the boat obviously wouldn't make such good progress upwind. Beating to windward then is the balance between covering the best distance to windward and making the best speed. And it is the helmsman's skill in maintaining the fine line between them – especially in a fickle wind.

In pursuit of this and mindful of the ever-changing direction and strength of the wind, the helmsman must continually nose the boat's head up into the wind to see if she will sail any higher without losing speed. If she does show signs of slowing down then he must immediately *bear away* a little so she may regain her speed. However, it is not only by rudder movement that

Sailing close-hauled on
the starboard tack. . . .

. . . and on the port tack.

he makes the boat sail efficiently; he also needs to be ready to
trim his sails. Hardening them when the wind increases, easing
them when it fails.

A good helmsman becomes finely attuned to his boat and
can tell in an instant, without any instruments, whether she is
sailing well. You and I have to content ourselves with less
subtle signs. If the boat is being pinched then apart from the
shaking jib (or rather before it) we may also expect the bow
wave to become less audible; the forestay to sag; the boat to come
a little more upright and the weight on the tiller to decrease. If
the boat is being sailed too *free* she will heel more and the
weight on the tiller will probably increase. Incidentally, this
weight on the tiller is known as *weather helm* and results from
the boat continually trying to come up into the wind. It is

something which is deliberately 'built in' to the boat as a safety factor. That is to say that if for some reason or another the helmsman were to let go of the tiller the boat would automatically round up into the wind, stop, and regain her stability. Weather helm then should be present in all boats in all but the very quietest of conditions.

Beating to windward is a continual challenge and made all the more so by a wind that neither stays in the same place nor blows with the same strength all the time. And it is the anticipation of the changing wind, and the tactics to meet it, that is the essence of the helmsman's skill.

He does however, have things to help him. There are *telltales*, little pieces of ribbon hung on the shrouds; or the burgee, the flag at the top of the mast; or even instruments. All of these will give him the wind's direction relative to the movement of the boat. But as I have said a good helmsman must anticipate and for this he will need to look at the water around him, to see from the ripples or the spindrift from a wave whether the wind is suddenly increasing or having a directional change. Experienced helmsmen can even detect a change in the wind by feeling it on their arms and their face.

But if all this has made windward sailing sound too scientific, or too troublesome like a tough piece of gristle – you can chew but never swallow – take heart. It is really only in competition that you have to keep on top line. Stick an old long-keeled cruising boat on her windward leg one lunchtime and you'll hardly need touch her until breakfast the next day.

Another point about windward sailing in a larger boat is that there is no necessity for the crew to sit on the gunwale or lean out to counter-balance the heeling force of the wind on the sails. In a dinghy this is essential because the crew are the 'living ballast' and if they don't use their weight with expedience and rapidity the boat will probably capsize.

The ballast of a cruising boat comes in the form of a large lump of lead (or iron) nestled down into the keel. It is more than enough to keep the boat from capsizing no matter how much she may heel. Nevertheless it is sensible for the crew to sit on the windward side. Naturally in a very small cruiser it is important that they do so because their weight still represents a large part of the boat's stability and by sitting to windward they ensure that she sails efficiently on a reasonably even keel.

One final difference between windward sailing in a cruising boat and a dinghy is that in the dinghy the sheets are never made fast but always held in the hand. This is so they may be let go in an instant should the boat heel over to the point of capsize. (This, incidentally, is another safety factor and can even apply in a cruising boat if hit by a sudden and particularly heavy squall. If the boat seems threatened and heels alarmingly then immediately let the sheets *fly*!) But the otherwise comparative stateliness and stability of a cruiser relieves the crew of this anxiety and chore. In a cruiser the sheets are normally made fast – albeit temporarily!

Well we have been sailing on this *tack* for a couple of pages so now let's suppose that our destination lies directly upwind! If we continue to sail with the wind a mere 45 degrees on our bow – which is bravely the best we can do – then it won't be long before it becomes apparent that our best just ain't good enough. We shall have to resort to *tacking*.

Tacking is a method whereby the boat is made to make a series of zig-zag movements to journey upwind. It entails turning the boat through 90 degrees so that the wind may be brought from one bow onto the other, or in the vernacular, from one *tack* to the other. It also means that the wind will then blow on the other side of the sails and in the case of the jib this means passing the *clew* across to the other side of the boat by means of the jib sheets.

It is a manoeuvre which has to be carried out smartly while the boat carries plenty of headway. And sometimes, to give her that extra bit of speed, it helps to let her sail *free* for just a moment or two before tacking. For unless the boat has sufficient speed when she tacks she is likely to falter and lay like a dead thing with her bow stuck facing into the wind and all her sails a shakin' (ignominious though this sounds – they call it being in *irons* – it is a very useful and positive way to stop the boat should you suddenly run into trouble).

The order is given '*Standby to go about*' followed by '*Ready about . . .*' '*Lee O*'. On this final order the rudder is turned and the boat's head begins to come up into the wind. Throughout this action the crew must keep their heads down low watching

'In irons' the boat is pointing dead into the wind, her sails are shaking and were it not for an engine which is obviously pushing her along she would be making no progress. Bringing the boat into the wind like this is the quickest and most convenient way of stopping her. (Note: a boat proceeding under both sail and motor should carry the appropriate signal.)

Most skippers like their crews to sit up to windward. . . .

out for items of rigging which may flog and in particular the boom as it swings from one side of the boat to the other. They should in fact be down in the middle preparing to shift their weight to the other side – rather an essential part of the operation in a dinghy as has already been pointed out.

When the boat's head is facing into the wind the jib sheet is let go and the slack taken in on the jib sheet on the other side of the boat. By the time the boat has *paid off* on her new tack this new jib sheet will have been hauled in tight. By this time also the helmsman will have corrected the swing of the boat so that no time is lost before she is settled and sailing on her new tack and as near to the wind as he can get her.

So far I have described beating to windward, or sailing *close hauled* as it is sometimes called. But now let's imagine that after a series of tacks we decide to *bear away* and sail with the wind on a much wider angle on our bow. We could of course do this by the action of the rudder alone but if this were done, with the sails still pinned in hard, then the pressure of the wind would be continually trying to 'spin' the boat back into the wind. In other words you would have to fight this tendency with the tiller and the boat would become very heavy on the helm, she would also heel excessively. The obvious thing to do then is to ease the sheets as well and allow the sails to swing further out. This brings us to the next point of sailing which is known as *reaching*.

To be correct it is called reaching when the wind is still before the beam, but directly the wind is brought abaft the beam then the boat is said to be *broad reaching*.

Broad reaching is most people's favourite sailing position, when very often the best speeds are attained. And because you are sailing with the wind, and the waves behind you, it tends to be warmer, smoother and a good deal drier than when sailing into the wind. If sailing ships could have always broad reached their way between ports then steamships would never have been invented.

When the boat is broad reaching the sheets are eased still more and as a result the main boom, naturally, swings further out. Unfortunately it not only swings out, but it also rides up, which in turn causes the mainsail to belly in the middle and develop a twist. It still may appear to be drawing well but if you were able to stand off and view it you would notice that it is *spilling* wind at the top. To prevent this happening most boats are fitted with a *boom vang* or *kicking strap* which secured to the underside of the boom at the fore end stops it from riding up.

It may be that by now you are contentedly sat back, you have eased the mainsheet to its uttermost and are beginning to agree that broad reaching is a very enjoyable point of sailing. Then suddenly you look up and notice the jib has collapsed, it's not pulling any more. You are now on a new point of sailing, you are *running* or *running before the wind* as it is properly called. The wind is now somewhere between dead astern and two points on the quarter, your mainsail is boomed out as far as it will go and it's shielding the wind from the jib. It is time for you to sit up.

To begin with the jib is not doing its job and the boat is therefore not moving so quickly. You can remedy this in one of two ways: either by pulling in the mainsheet, moving the tiller and getting back onto a broad reach, or by setting the jib on the other side of the boat where it is clear of the mainsail altogether. This is called sailing *wing a' wing*. In this position the centreboard is lifted almost completely up. In a strong wind, and more especially with a cruising boat not bent on making the best speed, it is sometimes a good policy to drop the mainsail and run under the jib. This is much more comfortable and less troublesome, as will become clear in a moment.

Running dead before the wind seldom pays dividends. It is slower and the boat is more inclined to roll. In a rough sea she may *broach* – swing beam on to the waves and get out of control, while there is the ever present danger of an accidental gybe. This can happen through a sudden shift in the wind or as a result of inattentive steering when the wind – instead of blowing on the inside of the sail as it was before – suddenly comes round to blow on the outside. Then *whoosh* . . . before you know it the sail and boom have swung across to the other side of the boat with the speed of summer lightning. The effect of this boom colliding with a crew member en route is something best not to consider. Certainly it doesn't do the boat's rigging much good while in a small dinghy it could very easily result in a capsize. But it could be that your destination lies directly downwind and so how else are you going to get there other than by running? The answer is by *tacking downwind*, that is to say by making a zig-zag course going from one broad reach to another. True it does mean sailing a further distance, but this is more than compensated by the increased speed of broad reaching. Admittedly you can overdo this strategy and sail so far off the wind that the extra speed you gain no longer makes up for the extra distance. But if you sail just far enough off the wind to enable the jib to keep drawing, i.e. away from the blanketing effect of the mainsail, then this is a fairly good guideline.

The manoeuvre by which you turn the boat from one broad reach to the other by bringing the boat's stern through the wind is called . . . yes, gybing. However, there is nothing to fear provided it is done carefully in what is called a controlled gybe. Although having said that I must hasten to add that it is not something to recommend in really strong winds; in this instance it is better to drop the main and sail under the jib downwind.

The drill for gybing. The warning is given *Stand by to gybe* and on hearing this the crew will have to get down low in the boat and be sure their heads are clear of the boom; they will also have to let go the boom vang, if there is one rigged, and prepare the jib sheets for the next point of sailing. Meanwhile the helmsman will steer the boat so that her stern is brought close into the wind and at the same time take in all the slack of the mainsheet. He will continue to take in all the slack until the mainsail is drawn in tight. The purpose of this is so that when the wind does catch the sail on the other side, as it will shortly do, the hardened mainsheet will limit its travel. In other words the sail and boom cannot go rocketing across the other side of the boat nor high in the air, in short its movement is *controlled*.

On the order '*Gybe O*' the helmsman puts the helm firmly over and the boat's stern swings into the wind. Directly this happens, and it has to be a very definite movement of the rudder so the boat will not falter, the wind strikes the leeside on the mainsail, the helmsman frees the mainsheet and quickly and carefully allows the mainsail to run out on the other side. The crew meanwhile let go the jib sheet and set the jib on the other side. The boat is now broad reaching on her new course.

Those, very basically and with a great deal of variance from one boat to another, are the basic manoeuvres in sailing. If you plan to practise them alone in your own boat then choose a day when the wind is light. This is not a slight of your courage but old-fashioned logic; when the wind blows light, the boat sails slow . . . makes it so much easier to understand what is happening.

9 LEARNING THE ROPES

Odd when you think of the old-time sailing ships – which carried more string than a Bombay taxi – that there were hardly any ropes actually called by that name! The bolt *rope* around the edge of the sail, I think was the only exception. The word *rope* was as rare as a *Street* in the suburbs; they all had far more distinctive names.

Not because the sailor thought the word too common, affectation was never his complaint; simply that long experience had taught him that to tell a man to: 'Go and undo that bit of rope hanging from the mast . . .' was as dangerous as it was vague.

And so it has survived today. Collectively they can all be called ropes, but do remember sheets, warps, halyards, lanyards, topping lifts, they each have a specific name.

Once you have learnt the names you can then begin the process of taming and training, because ropes can be treacherously unpredictable at times. They can tangle; tie themselves in immovable knots; trip you up and even slide over the side and throttle your propeller if they've a mind. ALWAYS keep them neatly coiled, and if there is any danger that they may still get loose then make sure that the coil is secured.

Figure 7 demonstrates how to coil a rope in the hand. It is important to do this properly or the rope will not come away freely the next time you need to use it – in a hurry! But more than this it is the twisting of the rope with the right hand that rids the ropes of its twists and kinks which might otherwise damage it permanently.

If a rope is made fast to a cleat and you wish to coil the remaining tail, as with for example a halyard secured to the mast, then start the coil next to the cleat and work towards the free end. As explained, it is necessary to twist, and sometimes spin the rope when coiling and it is impossible to do this with the end made fast.

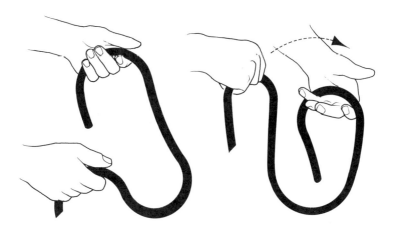

Fig 7 Coiling a rope in the hand
The coiling is done in a clockwise direction. Hold the end of the rope in the left hand. Bring up each new coil with the right hand giving it a half twist as you do. The 'coils' will then fall in place.

Ropes such as mooring warps, heaving lines, anchor cables etc., which are usually stowed in lockers, need to have their coils secured. This will prevent them falling apart and provides for a still neat coil when next you pull them out. The simplest way to secure a coil for stowage is with a *half-hitch* coil as shown in figure 8.

It happens that some ropes have to be coiled and secured in place, and again the halyard on the mast is a good example. For this the *halyard coil* shown in figure 9 is one of the most effective methods – although it has to be admitted, a piece of knicker elastic previously fixed to the mast is quicker.

If the rope you are handling has any weight on it then treat it with caution. This particularly applies when making a rope fast around a solid structure – as for example when heaving in the anchor cable and trying to catch a turn around the samson post, or when easing the fore-sheets from a cruiser's winch. In each case the weight on the rope is not constant: a sudden wave to lift the bow; a sudden puff of wind to fill the sail, both could double the loading on the rope and catch you unexpectedly. Keep your fingers out of the way! When making a rope fast where a weight is involved make sure they are never caught between the rope and the fitting; and when *surging* a rope,

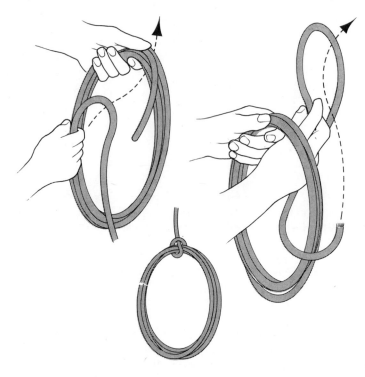

Fig 8 **The half-hitch coil**

Make a loop a little way from the end of the rope and pass this
through the middle of the coil. Take the end of the rope and
pass this over the top of the coil and in through the loop. Pull
the end tight, the half hitch that has been formed will then close
around the coil preventing it from falling apart.

that is to say easing it off, do so by checking the turns of rope
with the flat of your hand keeping fingers outstretched and
rigid – rather as you might do when handing a strange horse a
sugar knob (figure 13).

It has been said that when sailing a dinghy the sheets should
never be made fast but kept in the hand. This was actually
said in the previous chapter and a picture has suddenly come
to my mind of a wind-smitten, spray-sodden reader, fingers
torn and bleeding, still uncomplainingly carrying out the order.
Makes me feel like the man who set off the charge of the Light
Brigade.

It is permissible, *of course*, to take a single turn around a deck

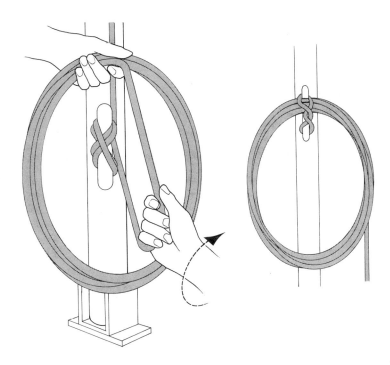

Fig 9 The halyard coil
Coil the end of the halyard in the usual way, starting with the
end next to the cleat. When the coil is complete pass the right
hand through the centre of the coil, grasp the cleated end of the
halyard and twist it a couple of times. Drop the top of this
twisted loop over the top of the cleat and the coil is then held
tight against the mast.

fitting. In a dinghy this will probably be with either one of the
three patent jam cleats shown in figure 14; notice their design
allows the rope to be freed in an instant. Alternatively a single
turn can be taken around the conventional cleat, although this
will not take all the weight nor, very probably, relieve you of
the need to keep hold of it.

If a rope is to be made fast to a cleat more or less permanently
– as for example with a cruiser's mainsheet, or the halyard in
the case of the dinghy – then it is important to begin the turns
with a complete round turn led first to the back of the cleat
(figure 15A). This ensures that if the rope has to be surged it
can be checked and kept under control. If a simple cross turn

69

Tailing a halyard winch. The operation of winching generally requires two people; one person to crank the winch handle and the other to *tail* or heave on the end of the rope. In the photograph the man on the tail has taken a turn with the rope around his hand; this is not recommended.

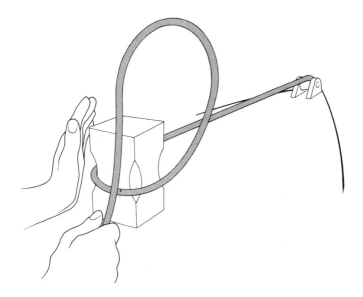

Fig 10 **Protection of fingers**
Snatching a turn on the anchor rope. A sudden wave or gust of
wind may double the weight on the rope. Keep the fingers clear.
Throw on another turn by twisting the hand; use the ball of the
other hand to check the rope while you do.

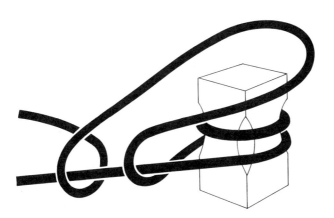

Fig 11 Making an anchor rope fast to samson post with a tug-boat
hitch. This is a quick way to hold the rope if there is a lot of
weight involved. If the rope is to be secured permanently, put
more round turns on top or another tug-boat hitch. This can
also be used with chain.

Fig 12 Surging a rope, or easing it out a little at a time from the winch. Keep several turns on to act as a brake. Ease the rope with one hand. Check with the ball of the other hand. Keep the fingers clear.

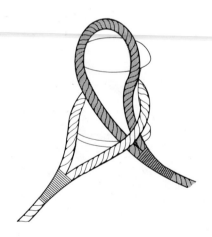

Fig 13 If the one and only bollard already has a rope on it be sure to dip your mooring line through the eye of it. This way both you and the other man can let go independently and without disturbing each other. A sensible precaution if he wants to sail at three o'clock in the morning!

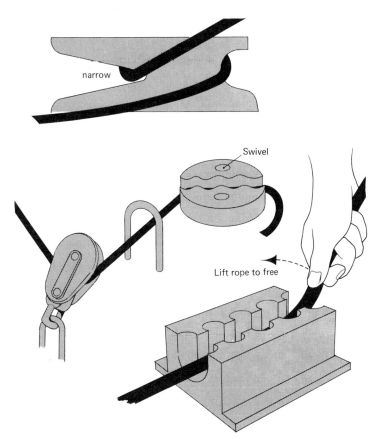

Fig 14 **Various patent jamming cleats**

were first put on there is a chance that the rope could flip off the horn of the cleat and take charge of itself.

Because cleats tend to be too small (or ropes too big) it is sometimes necessary to secure the figure-of-eight turns on a cleat with a slipped hitch (figure 15B). Make sure it is looped as the drawing shows for otherwise you may not be able to get it off in a hurry.

Strong sunlight, fungus and the mouse, that terrible trio that saw off so many good ropes when you and I were scouts cannot harm the modern synthetic rope. Nevertheless it does require some looking after. Do not allow kinks to develop, as they most certainly will if ropes are not kept coiled and tidy. If a rope does acquire a number of kinks or bad twists in the course of its duty then rid them either by spinning the rope or

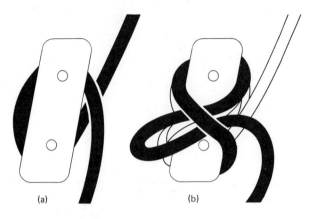

Fig 15 A The correct way to commence the turns on a cleat is with a round turn. This permits the rope to be surged without jamming. To make fast permanently continue with a number of figure-of-eight turns.

B Turns may be secured with a slipped hitch. Never use this for making fast sheets.

towing astern. Never, never try to get rid of the kink by pulling it out as this may severely damage the rope.

Make sure that ropes are not subject to bad nips, i.e. forced to run through, or over objects much less than three times their own diameter. This particularly applies to pulley wheels (known as *sheaves*) and undersized deck fittings. Failure to ensure this may result in the rope being crippled and its strength and length of life dramatically shortened.

Similarly, protect the rope from chafe. Do not allow it to rub against sharp edges. This is the unhappy fate of mooring ropes and it can be prevented either by slipping a section of plastic hose pipe over the rope, where it passes over the offending projection, or by *parcelling* the rope with canvas. Do not however, confuse the slight hairy surface that all synthetic ropes take on with the more fibrous look of chafe. The former is normal and is no evidence that the rope has suffered a loss of strength.

Sheets and halyards can be made to last far longer if their working areas – the parts which are frequently cleated or pass through blocks – can be shared equally by all sections of the rope. Occasionally turn them end for end or chop a little off one end – obviously there is a limit to the number of times

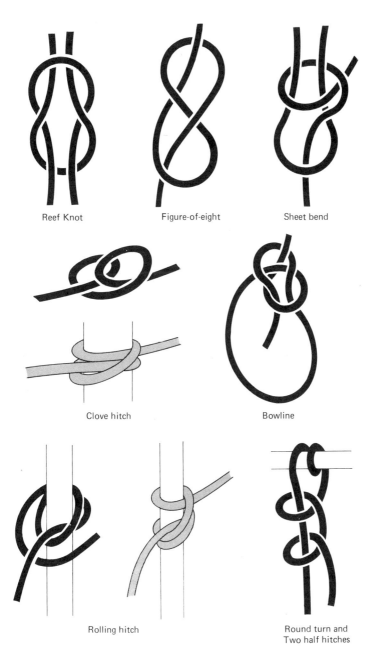

Reef Knot

Figure-of-eight

Sheet bend

Clove hitch

Bowline

Rolling hitch

Round turn and
Two half hitches

Fig 16 Bends and hitches

These basic knots are used every day aboard a boat; you cannot
afford not to know them. On the other hand you need not learn
any more!

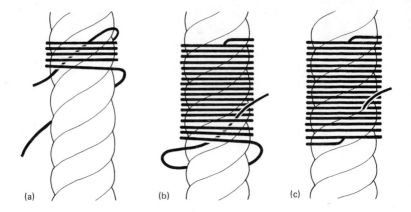

Fig 17 **The common whipping**
Begin by laying the end of the twine along the rope and then pass the turns tightly around it (a). In this way the end is anchored. The last couple of turns are left loose so that the other end of the twine may be passed underneath them (b). The turns are then worked tight, and the excess twine cut off.

you can do this! It also pays to give synthetic ropes a wash in fresh water. This helps to rid them of the salt which works its way into the fibres and makes the rope stiff. The best way to do this is to put them in a plastic bag filled with water and then swish them about.

Finally, look after the ends. It takes very little time for a fathom of rope to be lost if the end is not sealed and the strands and fibres are allowed to fall apart. Fortunately the fibres of synthetic ropes can be fused together by holding them over a match or slicing them through with a red hot knife. However, on a windy foredeck you can use more matches than a man struggling to light his first pipe and for these occasions you will need to resort to the time-honoured method of *whipping* (see figure 17). This is where the end of the rope is held tightly together by binding it with a length of sail twine. There are better methods than the one shown but this is the quickest and the most easily remembered.

10 BUOYAGE

Buoys are the street signs of the sea. They mark a whole variety of invisible items from wrecks to rocks; telegraph cables to target areas; sandbanks and sewers and other such unpalatable places. But perhaps their most popular function is to mark the channels where the deep water lies.

Not that this is an exclusive job for the buoys; in some places iron or wooden beacons are used, while in quieter places you will find the channel marked in a primitive way with bean sticks, or *withies* as they are called. But, be they buoys, beacons or bean sticks, the necessary requirement for all channel markers is that they should leave you in no doubt as to where the deep water lies, or more precisely, on which side you should pass them.

So to begin with they are divided into two groups: *port hand* marks and *starboard hand* marks – and it hardly seems worthwhile to add that port marks are left on the port side and starboard marks are left to starboard. However, this holds true only so long as a vessel enters a channel from seaward. Directly she turns around to come out again the whole picture changes; port marks are then left to starboard and starboard hand marks are left to port.

It isn't difficult for the sailor to cope with the transposition while he remains within a river or busy harbour. Here there is the lie of the land to guide him and probably a large volume of traffic to remind him as well. Where it does become difficult is offshore – and there are many areas of the world where channels are marked through shoal waters many miles off shore, the Goodwin Sands for example. Buoys are widely scattered in these lonely parts and the discovery of one by itself, which may belong to any one of a number of criss-crossing channels, can leave the beginner confused as to whether it should be left to port or to starboard.

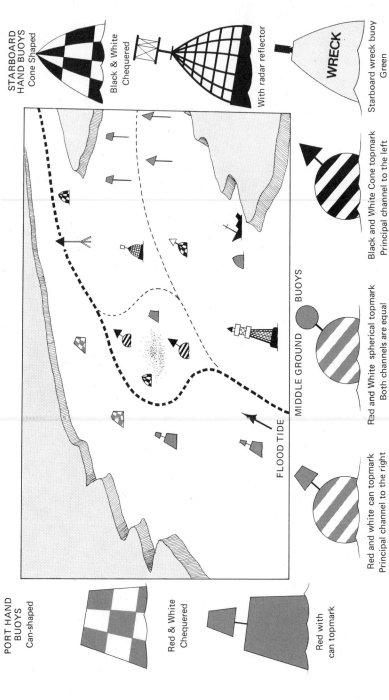

STARBOARD HAND BUOYS
Cone-Shaped

Black & White Chequered

With radar reflector

WRECK

Starboard wreck buoy
Green

Black and White Cone topmark
Principal channel to the left

MIDDLE GROUND BUOYS

Red and White spherical topmark
Both channels are equal

Red and white can topmark
Principal channel to the right

FLOOD TIDE

PORT HAND BUOYS
Can-shaped

Red & White Chequered

Red with can topmark

Fig 18 Marker buoys

It is the direction of the flood tide which provides the answer. With no land in sight this is the only thing which remains constant. In fact it probably happens that the tide runs directly up and down the channel which the buoy is marking (probably scours it anyway). And so it has been convened that the channel-marking system may be taken as 'correct' as long as the vessel is moving in the same direction as the main stream of flood tide.

So to understand the channel marks in the harbour or river you are entering it is necessary to know the direction of the flood. In practice it is simply a matter of remembering that, like you, it comes in from the sea.

Now that we have settled when a starboard hand buoy is a starboard hand buoy and when it is not, let's move on to their distinguishing features. Starboard hand buoys are painted black, or black and white chequered and are conical in shape. Port hand buoys are red, or red and white chequered and are flat-topped or can-shaped. Sometimes they are a solid welded construction and sometimes they have what looks like a parrot cage on top. The important thing is the colour and outline shape and it makes no difference how the latter has been arrived at.

To distinguish them one from another buoys may be given numbers, names, topmarks or lights. For it must be realized that not only do buoys mark the edges of channels but they are position indicators in their own right. The man sailing near the Goodwin Sands will use that buoy to find where he is. Similarly the man inching his way home through a well marked channel in fog, or at night will use each buoy to keep a check on his progress. Both will need to recognize each buoy so they can be identified on the chart.

The numbering of buoys is done in the usual custom of the sea with even numbers to port and odd numbers to starboard. The numbers start from seaward. Topmarks are shapes fixed above the body of the buoy and in the case of a starboard hand buoy they will either be a black cone or a black diamond – the latter is never used at the entrance of a channel. Port hand topmarks are either can-shaped or T-shaped, and again the latter is never used at the entrance of a channel. Topmarks should not be confused with radar reflectors which look like a lop-sided square and are fitted to make the buoy more 'visible' on a ship's radar screen. They are, however, useful for identification for whereas topmarks are rarely marked on the chart, radar reflectors always are.

Beacons and withies may also be fitted with topmarks although the latter are usually a primitive affair consisting of an upturned paint tin for a port hand mark and a triangular piece of plywood for a starboard hand mark – it looks like the prescribed *cone* from a distance but shrinks dramatically as you get nearer. In fact things in 'Gaswork Creek' are a bit frugal altogether and you have to be prepared for a few surprises. For example although the port hand withies may be red those on the starboard side could be green. The buoys too may be different. Instead of the usual pattern there may be only a single row of old beer barrels strung out to mark the centre of the channel. They may be painted, but as likely as not the only colour they'll have is what has been left there by the seagulls. In short, navigation in the backwaters of our world requires a little imagination.

But even in the principal channels things can be confusing. Very often there will only be a single row of mid-channel buoys to mark the existence of a channel. They are coloured with either red or white, or black or white vertical stripes. Then again, instead of an ordinary channel buoy to mark the seaward end of a channel there may be a *landfall* buoy with a tall lattice structure. These are to make the entrance of the channel more easily seen from the sea and similarly to give the light a greater height and therefore a greater range.

As suggested in the opening paragraph, there are many other types of buoys you will encounter, but perhaps the most important of the remaining are the *middle ground* buoys and *wreck marking* buoys. The former are used to mark the seaward and inner end of a sandbank that lies in mid-channel. They are sphere-shaped and have either red and white or black and white horizontal bands. Indeed it is the colour of these buoys and their topmarks which indicate which side of the divided channel has the deepest water. If, for example, the deeper water is on the left then the buoy will have black bands and a starboard topmark. And if the principal channel is to the right, then the buoy will have the colour and topmark of a port hand buoy. The buoy will also have red bands if the channels on each side are equal in size and depth; the only difference is the topmark which will be a red sphere at the seaward end and red cross at the inner end. Generally speaking small boats will be advised to take the minor channel where they will not be in the way or be bothered by bigger vessels.

Wreck marking buoys have the word 'Wreck' painted on them, they are green and if they show a light then that will be green also. Their shape will either be conical, can or spherical depending on whether the wreck lies, respectively, to the right, to the left, or in front of you.

Referring back to the identification buoys it is clear that one of the most positive ways to identify them is by their light – and it is to our advantage that buoy lights also shine through the day. Starboard hand buoys (or beacons) show a white light either as a single flash or in a series of three or five flashes grouped together with long periods of darkness interspaced between the groups of flashes. These are called *group flashing lights*.

Port hand buoys are also fitted with group flashing white lights but are even numbered two, four, or six. However, to increase their options they may instead show red lights in which case the numbers will be one, two, three, or four flashes.

The light signal from a buoy (or lightship, or lighthouse) follows a strict time pattern and to identify it you need to be able to count the seconds fairly accurately. Most people have their own pet way of doing this and there are those with exceptionally slow heart-beats who simply count their pulse.

It becomes even more difficult to count a group flashing light where you have two factors to contend with – the flashes and the period. One tip is to clench your fists (they probably are already), count the seconds and flick up a finger each time the light flashes. Then you stand bashfully to one side counting your fingers.

Once you have determined the light characteristic beyond all doubt, and it pays to check it a few times over, consult the chart for identification. The legend printed alongside the buoy, which is usually sketched in miniature, will naturally be abbreviated so that for example a port hand buoy showing four red flashes within a period of twenty seconds will read; Gp Fl (4) R. 20 sec. The chart will also denote the colour of the buoy and its name, if it has one.

Landfall buoys and middle ground buoys, to make them more distinctive, are very often fitted with *quick flashing* lights rather like a car's indicator. Sometimes these continuous series of flashes are interposed with short periods of darkness and in which case the light is described as *interrupted quick flashing*.

Another type of light you may see, although more commonly used by lighthouses and lightships, is the *occulting* light. This is best described as a steady light interrupted with periods of darkness. Often the periods of darkness are short like flashes and may even be grouped together. Such lights are called *group occulting* lights.

Before we leave the subject of buoys there are one or two points to remember. Firstly it can be very forbidding the first time you enter a strange harbour (or even a familiar one) at night and see a whole barrage of buoys winking at you; it looks like a pin ball machine gone crazy. The thing to do is to concentrate on the nearest buoy only. Identify it beyond all possible doubt – even get closer to it if you have to – and then, when you are perfectly sure where you are, check with the chart to see what the next buoy is flashing and start to look around for it – a compass course will help you. Only by following one buoy at a time will you be able to find your way in.

Another means by which buoys can be recognized is by their fog signal. Some of these, which may either be a bell, or a groaning siren, are activated by wave motion so on a calm day don't always expect to hear them.

Buoys are often placed in positions that are exposed to high winds and seas and so it sometimes happens that they drag their moorings. They should not always be relied upon implicitly. It happens too that because a buoy rides to a cable it can lie some distance downtide from its charted position at low water. It can even lie over the bank whose edge it is supposed to be marking!

And finally in complete contradiction to that well-intended warning, remember, if the wind or tide is pressing you hard so that you fear you will not clear a buoy safely, then don't try to; simply put your helm over and pass on the downwind or downtide side, there is almost certain to be sufficient water. And by the way, there is nothing mandatory about buoys; unlike road traffic bollards they are there only for your guidance.

11 THE HIGHWAY CODE

I think we can take it that when the maritime nations of the world sat down to draw up the International Regulation for the Prevention of Collision at Sea, they weren't really thinking about people like you and me. Nonetheless we are included; a little preamble in the front says: 'These rules shall be followed by all vessels upon the high seas and in all waters connected therewith.' While the word *vessels* is defined as: 'every description of water craft other than a seaplane.'

So they cover everywhere and everything from a Nagasaki sampan to the Woolwich Ferry . . . and it's comforting to think they would each know what to do in the unlikely event of a meeting.

These are not the only rules by which you must abide for there are also harbour regulations. Naturally they vary from place to place, but they are usually set out to cover such unsocial stunts as dumping your potato peelings over the side; water-skiing too near the beach or speeding and discharging oil into the harbour. In fact they are sensible laws designed to enhance the pleasure of sailing rather than impinge upon its freedom. In addition to these there are, for the man who wishes to race his boat, a large number of racing rules. However, as these would take a book by themselves to explain we'll return to the Collision Regulations, for that paradoxically is what they are usually called.

As you might expect in this atomic age the section that deals with sailing craft has shrunk like a teenager's jeans. All it says is:

'When two sailing vessels are meeting one another so as to avoid risk of collision, one of them shall keep out of the way of the other as follows:

i) When each has the wind on a different side, the vessel which has the wind on the port side shall keep out of the way of the other [see figure 19].

ii) When both have the wind on the same side, the vessel which is to windward (upwind) shall keep out of the way of the vessel which is to leeward (downwind) [see figure 20].

Fig 19 **Rights of way**

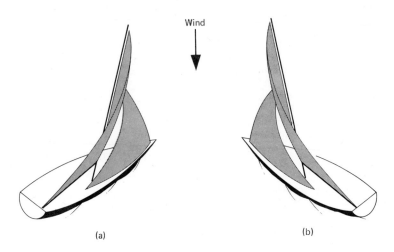

Wind

(a)   (b)

i) Both vessels sailing closehauled meeting with wind on different sides. Vessel A has the wind on the port side so she must give way.

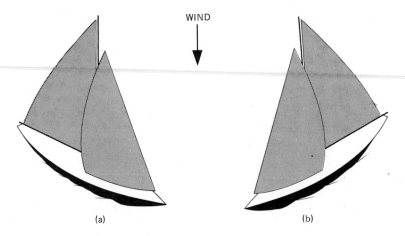

WIND

(a)   (b)

ii) Here the two meeting vessels are reaching but the same rule applies. They still have the wind on different sides so the vessel which has the wind on the port side (vessel A) must give way.

Important: If, in either of these examples, vessel B was in the process of overtaking vessel A and subsequently got into this situation then it is vessel B's responsibility to keep out of the way. Overtaking vessel *always* gives way.

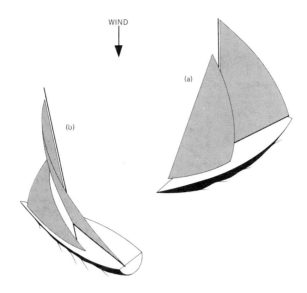

WIND

(a)

(b)

Fig 20 i) Here both vessels are meeting each other and both have the wind on the same side. However vessel A is upwind, she is the *windward* yacht and it is her responsibility to give way.

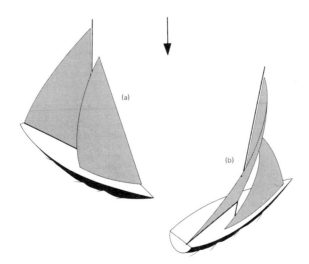

(a)

(b)

ii) In this example also both vessels have the wind on the same side, but still the windward vessel A must give way to B.

NB: Once again the overtaking rule applies. If, in each case, B had been overtaking and through bad handling had got into this position it still is her job to keep out of the way.

85

The rules do not state exactly what action you should take having been told to get out of the way, for it obviously depends on the circumstances. All they suggest is that avoiding action can be taken by either slackening speed, stopping or going into reverse. The suggestion is just one facet of the demise of the sailing ship for they are actually talking about motor ships – it is rather difficult to make a sailing ship go backwards, deliberately. However, it is fairly easy to slow a sailing boat or indeed stop her altogether. This is done by *luffing* or bringing the boat's head into the wind as was described in a previous chapter.

A more common method of avoiding collision is to alter course; either by bearing away or going about (tacking or gybing). But whatever you choose to do the law is emphatic that your action must be made in ample time, must be positive and leave the other chap in no doubt as to what you are doing. It is a good idea to exaggerate your action in the initial stage. One thing you must avoid is crossing his bow.

This completes the rules so far as two sailing vessels meeting are concerned, except for two important provisos. Firstly, a vessel overtaking another must always be prepared to give way. It doesn't matter what action the other boat takes – it can sheer wildly in front of the overtaking vessel's bow if it likes – the responsibility remains unchanged and it is the overtaking vessel's responsibility to keep out of the way right up until the moment she is well past and clear. The rule applies to all vessels so that even if you were able to puff your way past the QE2 it would still be your responsibility to keep out of the way.

Secondly it is important to remember that fishing vessels, when engaged in fishing and *under way* (that includes trawling, trolling or lying to drift nets) have absolute right of way. And no matter if they are sailing boats in an otherwise conceding situation, you must still keep clear of them.

Finally, the rules state very clearly that if a collision cannot be avoided by the action of the giving way vessel alone (which also means that if the giving way vessel does nothing at all) then it is your responsibility to take avoiding action also. In other words it will be no good standing up in court and telling the judge that it was the other chap's fault, he wasn't looking where he was going. In fact this seems a good place to put in the reminder that the sea is unforgiving; a man survives only by his skill and watchfulness and even the most watertight excuses won't help you.

Certainly this is never more true than in the small boat sailor's dealings with big ships. It used to be said that in all eventualities 'steam gives way to sail' and quite a number of staunch adherents have gone to an early grave with those words on their lips. But steam, or power of any description does not always give way to sail. It doesn't give way with respect to overtaking vessels; it doesn't give way where fishing craft are concerned and, to all intents and purposes, a ship will not give way to a sailing vessel in a narrow channel – here it is the sailing boat's responsibility to keep out of the way.

It is true that in the open sea a large vessel will endeavour to keep out of the way of a sailing yacht but before you can draw any comfort from this we ought to consider the limitations. A huge tanker proceeding at about 17 knots will stop in an emergency – it takes about six miles! Alternatively, she could put her rudder hard over to avoid you but, from the time you are first sighted until the turn commences she will have covered over a quarter of a mile! And when she does turn she needs a tremendous amount of sea room in which to swing. Perhaps even the little bit that you're sitting in! Another point to remember is that these extremely large ships may, in some areas of the world, be navigating with only a few feet of water under their keels. They cannot always deviate far from their set course without stranding themselves. But the final stark reality is that it is extremely difficult to see a small sailing boat from the bridge of a huge ship, especially at night. Moreover there is the disquieting fact that not all of these ships may keep an efficient look-out.

To summarize this point: expect only relatively small power driven vessels to give way to you, up to about the size of a coaster (coastal ships are very good in this respect). Do not get in the way of any ship, however small, while it is navigating a narrow channel. And finally keep clear of all large ships in the open sea and satisfy yourself that if they do come close they have seen you. (See the remarks in chapter 7.)

The Collision Regulations also state what lights a small sailing vessel is to carry. Briefly they are as follows: a green light has to be shown on the starboard side and a red light on

In narrow channels and confined waters the sailing boat no longer has 'right of way'.

the port side. Both of them must be visible for a distance of at least two miles. The lights must be fixed so that each is visible over an arc of the horizon of 112½ degrees of the compass, that is from right ahead to 22½ degrees (two points) abaft the beam on their respective sides. They can be oil or electric.

Naturally in small boats it is not always practical to fix these lights, in which case the rules allow you to carry a single lantern with red and green shades. It is called a combined lantern, it shows the light over the same recommended arcs and it has to be visible for at least one mile. If it is not possible actually to fix this lantern to the boat (say perhaps because of bad weather) then it must be kept ready to hand and shown in its right position and in good time, so that other vessels can see you. Small rowing boats and sailing dinghies need only carry a torch. Most sailing vessels are fitted with a white stern light, although this is not actually a requirement. It is sufficient to have ready to hand a torch that you can show so that an overtaking vessel can see you.

But don't stint yourself on lights; small sailing boats are very difficult to see at night especially when you remember that the heeling of the boat and the blanketing effect of the sails all but obscure the lights you are required to carry. There are an optional set of red and green lights which may be carried high up on the mast and these partly help to overcome the problem, but most practical seamen are agreed that the safest course is for a yachtsman to buy the biggest, most powerful flashlight he can afford to carry and show it in good time whenever the occasion demands.

When a vessel anchors at night (and strictly within the meaning of the rules this includes securing to a mooring buoy) she must show an all-round white light where it can best be seen and visible for at least two miles. During the day she is required to show a large black ball in place of the light which must be at least two feet in diameter. In practice most people hoist a fender.

Another shape which sailing craft are sometimes required to show is a black cone of similar dimensions. This is to be hoisted, point downwards, in the forward part of the vessel when she is proceeding under engine. It doesn't matter whether the sails are drawing or not; so long as they remain hoisted the signal must be shown. The idea of this is that other vessels will recognize that she is now a power-driven craft and therefore relinquishes all rights of way attributed to sailing vessels. She must behave as a power vessel, obey the rules for power vessels and even show the mandatory white steaming light above her sidelights.

Two final points covered by the rules are: that when navigating a channel you must keep to the starboard hand side (in other words you drive on the opposite side of the road to what we do in Great Britain) and the reminder that apart from the distress rockets and flares mentioned in chapter 7 one can also summon help by:

sounding your fog signal continuously

sending SOS by light (or radio)

slowly and repeatedly raising and lowering arms outstretched to either side

showing the international code signal for distress NC

exhibiting flames such as a paraffin soaked rag

showing a signal consisting of a square flag with a ball or circular shape either above or below it

firing a gun at minute intervals.

In conclusion it seems that many harbour authorities are beginning to tighten up on vessels, within their jurisdiction, that are found to be contravening Collision Regulations. Several offenders have been taken to court. It is therefore in your interest to understand the rules thoroughly, especially those which concern power craft. These are very simple and state in the first instance that if two power vessels are approaching each other end on, or nearly end on, so as to involve risk of collision, then each shall alter course to starboard so that each may pass down the port side of each other. This does not apply to vessels that are meeting on a seemingly converging course but will actually pass clear of each other, but only those that are likely to collide.

The second case is when two power vessels are on a crossing course and likely to collide. The rules state that the vessel which has the other on her own starboard side must keep out of the way of the other. Remember both these rules apply to sailing vessels which are proceeding with the aid of an engine.

The rules are printed in such publications as Reed's Nautical Almanac or they can be bought from HM Stationery Office as a separate publication.

12 THE UPS AND DOWNS OF SAILING

Tides, of course, do not concern us all. And while a chapter about them may be of passing interest to the Mediterranean sailor – who enjoys a slight rise and fall – it won't raise a flicker from a gravel pit sailor and, perish the thought, my entire Dead Sea readership will have already yawned and shut the book.

In point of fact they don't know what they're missing because tides put the sparkle into sailing. Consider the rich man racing his yacht in the Mediterranean. It doesn't matter what gadgets he has, what sails he puts up, how well the wind serves or how hard it blows – have a hurricane up his tail if he likes – he will never be able to equal the speed or feel the breath-taking exhilaration of the beginner unwittingly launching his boat in the Pentland Firth (two hours before high water Dover). He'll be screaming along at 10 knots before he has had a chance to get his sails up!

Even in the less turbulent waters of our coast, a 3-knot tide can, on occasions, double the speed of a small sailing yacht. Of course this assumes she is going with the tide – faced the other way she'd be stopped!

Then again if it were not for tides to raise the level of water now and then, how should we re-float the many thousands of boats that go aground each weekend? True, if the tides hadn't lowered the level in the first place they probably wouldn't have gone aground, but you can see it all makes for interest.

Before you launch your boat in your chosen location it is a good idea to view the place when the tide is out, or, to use the correct term, at *low water*. You won't be able to memorize every sandbank and hollow; besides your chart does that. But the suggestion is that after the shock of seeing such a wide expanse of mud or so many uncovered rocks where previously there had been blue, sparkling water, you'll never want to go afloat without consulting your *tide tables*.

A set of tide tables can be bought from a ship's chandler for a matter of pence. They will give you the times of high and low water with the heights of each tide printed alongside. Nothing could be more simple! At first glance they look more daunting than a railway time-table so let's begin with a little explanation.

Tides are much affected by local geography and if, for example, they have a wide expanse of flat ground to flood, or a series of narrow entrances to squeeze through, then this can upset their 'clock'. But by and large it takes about $6\frac{1}{4}$ hours for a tide to *flood*, or come in, and about $6\frac{1}{4}$ hours to *ebb*, or go out. This means that the time interval from one high water to the next (or one low water to the next) is roughly $12\frac{1}{2}$ hours. In other words the times of high and low water progress and come about half an hour later each day. But it isn't only the times of high and low water that change, the *heights* of the tide do likewise! (If they didn't you wouldn't need a set of tables.)

Tides, you must know, are caused by the gravitational pull on the waters of the earth by the moon. However, once a fortnight, for a brief spell, the sun joins in as well and the outcome of their combined strength is to raise the waters still higher. When this happens, and it is spread over a few days, the high waters are higher and the low waters are lower. The period over which it lasts is called *springs* and the big tides produced are called *spring tides*. (The word comes from the Norse language and means to 'swell' – it has nothing to do with the season.) Spring tides reach their peak two days after a new moon, and one day after a full moon, that is to say once a fortnight. They also vary in height throughout the year with the biggest tides coming at the time of the spring and autumn equinox.

Midway between the periods of these large tides come the smaller *neaps*. They have a smaller range and reach neither the same height nor the same low level as the spring tides do, although the mid-tide position for both remains the same.

So it can be seen that throughout the month, from one new moon to the next, the heights of the tide are continually changing, getting higher as they approach springs, getting smaller as they 'take off' towards neaps.

But the heights given in the tide table book are not an

indication of the depth at any particular spot – town quay steps, gaswork jetty or similar illustrious landmarks. The heights simply state how much 'extra' water there is to add to the amount already shown on the chart, a sort of bonus.

If you look at any chart you will see that the sea areas are covered with very small numbers. These refer to the depth of water at the places they mark – not a fish census as some old lady tried to tell me. They are called *soundings* and it is important to establish at the outset what measurement they represent. That is to say are they feet, fathoms or metres? Large scale charts such as those that show the plans of harbours were formerly marked in feet, while off-shore areas were marked in fathoms, or units of six feet; latterly all charts have been marked in metres.

These soundings nowadays represent the depth that existed on the lowest tide of the year. In other words they show the very minimum amount of water that you would be likely to find, discounting freakish conditions. It is, of course, a very sensible arrangement providing us with a moderately large 'safety factor'. However, there is a drawback in that when the chart shows a rock as being visible it means that it is visible only for half an hour at the time of the lowest tide of the year. For the remainder of the time, it is submerged but dangerously close to the surface. The depths and the heights that are recorded are known as the datum of the chart, or more familiarly, *chart datum*.

So, if you plan to sail down river and wish to know the depth of water on the harbour bar then all you need do is to look at the chart, read off the soundings, add the height given in the tables and that's what the depth of water will be.

But unfortunately, as you must realize, the only time when you can compute the depth so simply is when your departure coincides with the times of high or low water, for these are the only two heights given. At all other times you will need to calculate.

Unfortunately again, it isn't as straightforward as that; tides do not run at a constant rate and so you cannot for example say that one hour after HW the tide will have dropped one-sixth of its range; in reality it's hardly got started!

Like a lot of other things in this life, tides are a little late to get going each day and prefer to round off their working hours gradually. There is a 'rule-of-thumb' that equates to this and can be used quite effectively to find the height of the tide at any hour. It is called the *Twelfths Rule* and it is based on the assumption that the tide rises (or falls) one-twelfth of its total range in the first and last hour. It is set out like this:

Hour	*Rise or Fall*
first	1 twelfth
second	2 twelfths
third	3 twelfths
fourth	3 twelfths
fifth	2 twelfths
sixth	1 twelfth.

Remembered easily by the sequence 1, 2, 3, 3, 2, 1.

To work this rule one has first to find the *range* of the tide for the particular period in which you wish to sail, i.e. the difference in height between the last high or low water, and the next high or low water. The range is then divided by twelve. Here is a very simple example:

If HW is at 0800 hrs and the height is given as 18 feet, and if LW is at 1400 hrs and the height is 6 feet, how high will the tide be at 1200 hrs?

$$Range = 18 \text{ feet} - 6 \text{ feet} = 12 \text{ feet}$$

In first hour tide falls 1/12th of 12 feet = 1 foot
In second ,, ,, ,, 2/12ths of 12 feet = 2 feet
In third hour ,, ,, 3/12ths of 12 feet = 3 feet
In fourth hour ,, 3/12ths of 12 feet = 3 feet

Total = 9 feet

Height of tide at 1200 hours is $18 - 9 = 9$ feet.

It must be said that this rule is only correct during the bigger spring tides when the tide drops to somewhere near the level of water shown on the chart. For the rest of the time it suggests that there is far less water than there actually is, but as it errs well on the side of safety we can forgive and forget all about that.

One final point about the heights of tide which appear in the tables is that they can be quite remarkably changed by the weather; so also can the times. If the barometric pressure is high then this seems to weigh heavy on the water and it rarely comes up to its expected height. Conversely, if the pressure is low then the tide level may be very much higher. As a general rule it is reckoned that 1 inch of pressure can alter the height of a tide by a foot.

Heavy rain, or snow melting into rivers, can also increase the height of water in an estuary and this naturally affects the level of tide. But perhaps the most notable effect of all is that brought on by the wind. A strong wind blowing for a long period in the same direction as the flow of tide causes the water to 'heap up' – especially when it is trapped within a wedge of land. In contrast a wind blowing against the flow will hold it back so that not only does the tide not reach its predicted height but the times of high and low water are later.

But tides not only go up and down, they also swish from place to place. And as was mentioned at the beginning of this chapter, sometimes at a *rate* equal to, or even greater than the speed of a boat. Such a motive power is clearly something for the small boat sailor to reckon with.

Obviously the strength of these streams corresponds with the rise and fall of the tide and so the rate is weak during the first and last hours of a tide – but very strong during the middle hours. The rates also vary in springs and neaps and generally run twice as fast during springs as in neaps. Furthermore, they are affected by local conditions and geography, being strong in some places and weak in others. (This is explained in the next chapters.)

However, all these variations were simplified for the sailor with the advent of the *Tidal Atlas*. This is simply a map (actually a series of twelve maps all of the same area) which, with the aid of a generous sprinkling of arrows shows hour by hour the *set* or direction of the tide and its approximate strength for every part of the area covered.

Tidal atlases can be bought as a separate publication although a variation of them does appear on British Admiralty charts; in this case it is not pictorial. Stamford's Yachtsmen's Charts have tidal atlases reproduced in their margins.

I have said that the atlas gives an hour by hour description of tides' movement from one HW through to the next; still it must be clear that this has to refer to the HW at some specific place otherwise the information becomes ambiguous.

For this reason a 'standard port' is chosen and the HW times shown on the atlas will refer to that. The principal 'standard port' for the British Isles is Dover and if you plan to make cruises up and down the coast you will need a set of Dover tide tables (alternatively they are printed daily by some national newspapers). But it isn't only to be able to use the tidal atlases that a Dover tide table will be necessary, a great deal more tidal information is also based on it. For example, guidance on when is the best time to enter or leave a port in respect of having sufficient water or gaining advantage from the tidal set, is also made with reference to Dover. While local HWS are invariably given as occurring so many hours before or after HW Dover. Even those local tide tables mentioned at the beginning of the chapter were probably compiled from the time difference between HW at that place and Dover. In fact, so long as you know what the time difference is you could almost go without buying a set of local tide tables and make do with those of Dover.

I could have told you that a couple of pages back, but just think of the confusion it would have created!

13 TROUBLED WATERS

Apart from being a long way from home there is certain comfort in sailing far out to the ocean. Discount the possibility of being charged by a killer whale and you could safely say that changes are undramatic, that one patch of water will be the same as another. While the changes that do occur are borne on the wind and you'll know pretty soon by the feel of it whether it's a good day for taking your wristwatch to pieces or whether you'll spend most of the day standing on your head.

Other than a change in the wind there is nothing to upset the steady pattern of things. The wind isn't deflected or funnelled by mountains; the waves aren't suddenly wheeled around or tripped up by subterranean banks; they are not constricted by land nor are they reflected by high cliffs and walls; there is no tidal stream to upset and anger them, no sudden depths to tumble into, in fact nothing at all but mile upon mile of untroubled landscape where they can just glide on and on. (I don't know why more beginners don't begin their sailing out there.)

Around the coast it is different, waves alter and change their character, while the wind can shift and twist and blow quite suddenly from anywhere. You'll need your wits about you far more in coastal waters, where 90 per cent of all marine casualties occur.

A gloomy start, but it is important to realize that in coastal waters the sea isn't always as good as it looks. Without any alteration in the wind the sea can change in an instant and it is never exactly the same from one place to the next. There is no mystery in this; despite what the poets tell you, the sea is not a creature of moods. But with a forecast of the wind, a set of tide tables, a chart, a little knowledge and common sense you will be able to predict the changes and know fully what to expect.

Let's begin with the wind against tide situation. Imagine you are sailing in a wide river estuary. The tide is flooding into the river mouth and the wind is blowing that way too. The wind feels moderately strong but not unkindly and because the waves are very small you feel perfectly relaxed. In short it is excellent sailing weather. Then gradually you notice the waves are building up, which is odd, because the wind is still the same as it was. Within an hour the sea is quite rough, the spray is flying, the boat now needs bailing, you're wet and you're frightened and you're wondering what's happened . . . was it something you said?

What has happened is that the tide has turned against the wind. Previously the wind, blowing the same way as the tide, had the effect of smoothing out the waves. But now that the tide has turned against the wind, the waves are being whipped up. Moreover the ebbing tide, backed by the natural flow of the river and the huge reserves of water beyond, is much stronger and flows much faster than the flooding tide of an hour or so back.

So then, without any increase at all in the wind, this still moderate 3-knot tide has effectively turned a 12-knot breeze into a 20-knot wind, and produced waves a good 4 to 5 feet high.

The moral of this is to study the tide tables and the tidal atlas *before* you set out. If they indicate a strong tidal set against the present wind during the time you are out then you must know what to expect.

I have implied in the above description that 4- to 5-feet waves might be considered dangerous to a small boat; normally they're not. No, the point about these wind-against-tide waves is that they are usually short and steep, almost as if they have been squeezed up. They present no great hazard for the average cruising boat – although it would be very uncomfortable and wet, but more at risk is the small open dinghy with the ever-present chance that she might fill up.

It's a mistake some beginners make to believe that if they stick well inshore when making a passage they will be relatively safe – a sort of apron string mentality. In fact the reverse is true and the danger (if any) actually increases as they get closer to the shore, and near headlands in particular.

Headlands are the bits that the sea hasn't yet managed to wear away and it's because of this that they come in for special attention. Waves concentrate on a headland and are much steeper here than they are in the bays where they soon diffuse and lose their height. But wave intensity apart, the reason for treating headlands with caution has more to do with the tides.

The inner side of a tidal stream moving along a coast will naturally try to follow that coast and sweep in and out of the bays. The main stream meanwhile continues its unswerving course and meets this inshore stream every so often at a headland where it is swilling out from a bay. This meeting results in a marked amount of water turbulence and confusion which is made all the more so if the bay is particularly large or the headland particularly bold. Thus the inshore stream has had a good long run and collides with the mainstream at ninety degrees. The boiling, angry waves that grow out of this are referred to as *overfalls* although they might be locally known as 'the Race'.

Every headland has overfalls to some extent although not all

A dangerous sea on a sandbank. Notice that because the water is shallow the waves are breaking and sweeping in different directions. Keep clear of shallow water in rough weather.

of them are present for each hour of the tide and quite a few are considered so inconsequential that they don't even appear on the chart. Those that are shown on a chart may be taken to be hazardous to small boats in anything but settled conditions. For wind-blown waves entering a race will join in the mêlée and throw a boat drunkenly in all directions, they may even overwhelm her.

A race is obviously at its most dangerous during rough weather and during the middle hours of the tide when the streams are running at their strongest. For this reason also they are more dangerous at 'springs'. While one final point to remember is that they change their location with the ebb and flood tide.

It has been said that overfalls are caused by the directions of two tidal streams bumping into each other, but there are other contributory factors. For example, because of its constricting shape the tides run very much faster past a headland and can well exceed two or three times the rate of the tide in the bays. This obviously aggravates the already turbulent situation besides making it very difficult for a sailing boat in close vicinity to a headland to make progress against the tide.

There is also the geography of the headland to consider. The erosive effect of the sea on a headland is directed principally at sea level. So although there may be very little of the headland left standing it can still be there under the surface. It usually presents itself in the shape of rocks – in themselves a danger, but imagine the obstructive effect this large undersea wall has on the passing tide! Indeed it acts like a subterranean weir deflecting water up to the surface where it adds to the turbulence still further.

In short, keep away from headlands in all but the most settled weather!

Another localized trouble spot is the narrow entrance which forms the opening to a large natural harbour or inner sea. It's the neck of the hour glass through which an immense volume of tidal water is forced. A strong wind-against-tide situation may make such an entrance dangerous to small boats but of more common concern is the rush of the water itself.

There are places where the tide races out of the entrance at

Even in settled conditions an 8-knot tidal stream can present its problems and it is no place to be in bad weather. Sound of Scarba, Scotland.

speeds of 7 or 8 knots – making inward navigation impossible and outward navigation just a matter of holding your breath. But even the more usual rates of 5 or 4 knots can look awesome when the water boils and gurgles, taking on a sinister, evil look like a giant witches' cauldron. However, for all its appearances it isn't necessarily dangerous. Obviously you wouldn't want to fall in and for this reason dinghy sailors especially should navigate these entrances with extreme care, keeping down low in the boat and, as always, wearing their life-jackets. But the main thing to realize when sailing in a current like this is that things are very much taken out of your hands and it is the tide that is in control. You cannot easily stop or turn around, nor will you very easily be able to avoid the objects that come in your path. So in other words pick your time when coming through; make sure, if there is insufficient wind for you to control the boat, that you have plenty of room and remember the strongest current lies in mid-stream. This is a good point to remember when coming in against the tide; if you keep to the edges you will find the going very much easier and may even tumble across a *reverse* current to carry you through – for such is the peculiarity of tides.

In light weather the only concern you may have for the depth of water you are in is that it will be sufficient to support you. Providing this condition is met there is absolutely no risk in taking short cuts across offshore sandbanks or even coming in close to the beach if you want to. For dinghy sailors who may have to launch off a beach it will be quite natural to do so. But when the wind gets up the position changes and waves build up much steeper than they do in deeper water.

The height of a wave is very much determined by the depth of water beneath it. If there is a generous depth the wave can roll along unimpeded but if the water is shallow, then the 'foot' of the wave tends to drag on the bottom and its speed is slowed considerably. However, because the same volume of water is retained within the wave, and the same strength also, it takes on a different shape and grows very much taller.

You can see a good demonstration of this on a beach (and it's no bad thing for a sailing man to stand and watch the sea, witness the power of the waves, listen to them sucking their teeth). Beyond the surf the waves may be little more than gentle hummocks, but notice how they change as they come into shore. They steepen, slow down and crowd up on each other till finally they become so unstable they break!

This is, of course, an extreme example but a very convincing proof.

But there is something else. You cannot fail to have noticed that no matter where you stand on a beach – and it would be the same even if you were able to stand on four different beaches at once – that the waves always appear parallel to the beach. This is due to refraction, or the bending of the waves. What happens is that a pattern of waves travelling past the coast will suddenly feel their inner ends come under the influence of the shallow water. This, as we have seen, tends to slow them up and as a result the entire length of the wave front is wheeled around through 90 degrees to face the shore.

Exactly the same thing happens on an off-shore sandbank, even though it may be completely covered with water. However, here it becomes more complex because being exposed on all sides the bank is assailed with several wave patterns all criss-crossing together. This makes for a very confused and dangerous sea upon the bank with pyramid waves building up to a height several times those around them.

Still, there is no need to dwell on the misery, sufficient to say that in rough weather avoid the temptation of taking short cuts across sandbanks and, wherever there is a great variation in depth, keep in the deepest water.

Now, just to round off this gloomy section on sudden and isolated dangers we have the most important of all – the condition on the harbour *bar*!

The harbour bar is the name given to the inevitable sandbank that has formed at the entrance of any large natural harbour or river. It has grown from the deposits of sand and silt carried by the outflowing water which it usually spreads around so effectively that there is no way in or out of the harbour without crossing over it.

As can be imagined from its description and position, a bar will, at some time or another entertain most, if not all of the unhappy phenomena already described. It also has one extra hazard of its own. This is called *swell*.

A swell is the name given to a continuous procession of long rolling waves, a legacy of a long-forgotten ocean storm, that travel on majestically for hundreds of miles rounding off their edges to finally wind up on somebody's beach, whereupon they're called *surf beat* – if you're a surfer.

Away from the shore they represent no hazard to a man in a small boat unless . . . unless he happens to be crossing a bar at the time. Then the lower part of the swell, the *trough*, can dramatically reduce the already shallow water and deliver his bottom a nasty bump on the sand.

A swell can be present in otherwise quite calm conditions, although strangely enough it isn't always easy to detect out at sea, you may need to study the shoreline and watch the heaving of the sea to see if it's present. So remember, when attempting to cross the bar with a ground swell running, be sure to satisfy yourself that there is sufficient water over the bar for both you *and* the swell. Naturally you must make the same consideration with ordinary waves as well.

I hesitate to hark back on all the aforementioned miseries –

besides it has been said that an audience only takes in a limited amount of doom before they 'tune out' altogether. Nonetheless, it must be clear from what has been said that such a sandbank lying in shallow water at the entrance of a large harbour and exposed to fierce tides can really put on quite a show when a strong wind blows. Treat the harbour bar then with caution, remembering that conditions upon it can change by the hour and they needn't necessarily reflect the sea conditions elsewhere. The very worst time will be when a strong onshore wind meets an ebbing spring tide and should you have the misfortune to arrive off the port at just such a time it will be wise to delay your entry for a couple of hours until the tide has slackened or turned. Finally, remember that from seaward you are looking across the backs of the breaking seas so you won't see their wicked side until you are in amongst them – by when of course it will be too late and you'll be committed.

So far I have described the sea's accident *black spots*, for that's how they should be seen, small areas of occasional danger that, compared with the whole, are few and far between. Don't let the knowledge of them spoil your sailing nor keep you in harbour when there is a good breeze to enjoy.

It is only in certain conditions of wind and tide that they will be dangerous and most of the time you'll be able to sail blithely by listening to the cricket score and munching your sandwiches. But on these occasions try to think of how things *might* have been, how fortunate you are to have the *right* wind, the *right* tide and the *right* depth of water . . . you know, just to get used to the idea!

Now to talk about the all-over effect of weather, or more precisely wind. Some sailing people will claim that their utter dependency on the winds has brought them in close accordance with nature and they have only to look at the clouds or sniff the air to tell you what changes there'll be. Other people tap barometers – and usually with such bristling self-confidence that the six hours' weather either telescopes into the flick of a needle, or the instrument falls off the wall. The rest of us who have yet to develop these ancillary skills will listen to the BBC shipping forecasts.

The *Shipping Forecast*, as it is more generally known, divides the waters of the British Isles into areas and for each of these it gives the forecast for the next twenty-four hours. It is true to say that these tend to be far more bleak than the weather, or in other words that the wind is rarely as strong as the meteorologists predict. Most people accept this, realize the very difficult job they have and understand that they must err on the side of safety. Other people say they lie in their teeth.

The wind is known by two factors: *direction and strength* and one is just as important as the other. Direction is given as a compass point and refers to the direction that the wind comes *from*. (This, you will notice is contrary to tidal direction which indicates the direction in which the tide is setting.) The strength of the wind was categorized years ago by Admiral Beaufort who got the idea from someone else – but I won't say any more on either count, figure 21 on page 106 being plain enough. Force six should be taken as the limit for most boats and certainly for beginners.

But now having made that pronouncement I need to make the obvious distinction that a force six wind blowing off the land will not pose anything like the threat of an equivalent wind from the sea – especially if that wind has been blowing for a long period and has enjoyed a long, uninterrupted passage, or what is called a long *fetch*. Such a wind will be able to build up very big waves that may continue after the wind has died. It is clear then, that before putting to sea you will need to know not only the forecast of weather, but also what has gone before. Then you will need to think about local geography.

Because the wind needs a good fetch to build up waves, it is obvious that sailing directly under the land in an offshore wind will be reasonably comfortable and safe. Also the coast itself will have a shielding effect and the bite of the wind will not be felt. But now try to imagine the reverse of this situation with a very strong wind and sea beating against an exposed shore. This is known as the *lee shore* – a sort of back-to-the-wall situation. In the days of the large sailing ships, which were unable to sail much better than six points into the wind, the lee shore was the inescapable trap feared more than all. It accounted for far the greatest number of losses and, in fact, towards the middle of the nineteenth century the exposed coasts of Britain, notorious lee shores, were netting up to three new wrecks every day! In salvage terms the wrecks might have been described as an

Beaufort Number.	†Limits of Wind Speed in knots.	Descriptive Terms.	Sea Criterion.	Probable Height of Waves in metres and feet.*	Probable Maximum Wave Height in metres and feet.*
0	Less than 1	Calm	Sea like a mirror	—	—
1	1–3	Light air	Ripples with the appearance of scales are formed but without foam crests.	0·1 m $\frac{1}{4}'$	0·1 m —
2	4–6	Light breeze	Small wavelets, still short but more pronounced. Crests have a glassy appearance and do not break.	0·2 m $\frac{1}{2}'$	0·3 m 1'
3	7–10	Gentle breeze	Large wavelets. Crests begin to break. Foam of glassy appearance. Perhaps scattered white horses.	0·6 m 2'	1 m 3'
4	11–16	Moderate breeze	Small waves, becoming longer: fairly frequent horses.	1 m $3\frac{1}{2}'$	1·5 m 5'
5	17–21	Fresh breeze	Moderate waves, taking a more pronounced long form; many white horses are formed. (Chance of some spray.)	2 m 6'	2·5 m $8\frac{1}{2}'$
6	22–27	Strong breeze	Large waves begin to form; the white foam crests are more extensive eveywherre (probably some spray).	3 m $9\frac{1}{2}'$	4 m 13'
7	28–33	Near gale	Sea heaps up and white foam from breaking waves begins to be blown in streaks along the direction of the wind.	4 m $13\frac{1}{2}'$	5·5 m 19'
8	34–40	Gale	Moderately high waves of greater length; edges of crests begin to break into spindrift. The foam is blown in well-marked streaks along the direction of the wind.	5·5 m 18'	7·5 m 25'
9	41–47	Strong gale	High waves. Dense streaks of foam along the direction of the wind. Crests of wave begin to topple, tumble and roll over. Spray may affect visibility.	7 m 23'	10 m 32'
10	48–55	Storm	Very high waves with long overhanging crests. The resulting foam in great patches is blown in dense white streaks along the direction of the wind. On the whole the surface of the sea takes a white appearance. The tumbling of the sea becomes heavy and shocklike. Visibility affected.	9 m 29'	12·5 m 41'
11	56–63	Violent storm	Exceptionally high waves. (Small and medium-sized ships might be for a time lost to view behind the waves.) The sea is completely covered with long white patches of foam lying along the direction of the wind. Everywhere the edges of the wave crests are blown into froth. Visibility affected.	11·5 m 37'	16 m 52'
12	64+	Hurricane	The air is filled with foam and spray. Sea completely white with driving spray· visibility very seriously affected.	14 m 45'	—

Fig 21 **Beaufort wind scale**

The emergency services should not be abused but here was a
genuine need. The boat in question had been caught
unprepared and blown onto a lee shore.

'invisible export' or a natural resource, except that most of
them were ours anyway.

In theory the lee shore should present far less danger to the
modern sailing boat as she is able to point much higher into
the wind and therefore escape. But in practice the small *family*
cruiser performs poorly when pressed into a strong wind and
steep sea (as it will be in shallow water) and her predicament
is equally as grim.

The dinghy sailor, operating from a beach, would naturally
have beached his boat long ago, or even more sensibly, not
have ventured out through the surf in the first place. But the
cruiser owner must never think of beaching *his* boat as an
alternative solution for it would almost certainly result in the
loss of his boat, or the lives of him or his crew. If getting off a
lee shore has proved impossible, even with the aid of the engine,
then make as good offing as you can and let go the anchor.

107

In fact let go every anchor you have – and as much cable as you are able to veer. Then, unless the weather is definitely moderating, fire off your distress flares while it is still possible for the lifeboat to get alongside you

The mention of this reminds me that I have not advised a course of safe action should you find yourself in some of the other described situations. One hesitates to do this because each may demand a different action, while again the action recommended may vary from boat to boat. But let's take, for example, the probability of being swept into a race. The point to remember here is that things will happen fast; the boat will be thrown about violently and as the dominant force will probably be the tidal stream (rather than the wind) the control of the boat may be wrested from you. One thing is certain the experience will not last long – the strong tide will soon carry you through to the other side. Do not attempt to lower or shorten sail, there isn't time, in fact don't move around the boat at all but get down as low as you can and hold on. If the boat is a cruiser (which is more likely since a dinghy would not be out in these conditions), it may be advisable to let fly the sheets quickly, get down below and close the hatch leaving the naturally buoyant shape of the boat to carry you through. But this is a last ditch recommendation which you may also need to resort to in other extreme situations, although hopefully then you would have time to lower and lash the sails.

One case where this course of action is definitely *not* recommended is when shooting the harbour bar from seaward: here the boat must be kept moving ahead at all costs. Obviously it is better not to try at all, but if you should find yourself caught on a bar remember the biggest danger (apart from grounding on the entrance sides) is from the breaking crests behind you which may lift the boat's stern and swing it through 90 degrees. This is called *broaching* and the risk is that a second wave may strike while you lie in this helpless, perhaps flooded, condition. Lifeboats, which sometimes have to come over the bar as a part of their normal duties, are equipped with drogues which they tow behind to keep their stern into the sea and prevent them broaching. But they take some skill in their operation and besides, many people say they are impractical for yachts. The suggested action here is for them to simply keep moving ahead which is best achieved by lowering the mainsail in a heap and running in under the jib.

BAD WEATHER SAILING IN GENERAL

In your first year or so confine your sailing to fine or moderate weather only. Don't go too far offshore, except in very settled conditions, and if you are persuaded to make a long coastal trip then try to arrange it so that there are a number of ports which you could run into along the way. Learn to reef your boat, first in harbour and while under way (see chapter 14) and remember to always shorten sail in plenty of time and before the wind gets too strong. Alternatively, do not reef so severely that the boat will not sail properly. Listen to the shipping forecasts before you set out and while under way. Watch the sky (and barometer) for obvious signs of bad weather and remember that in port you can get a current and local forecast of wind and sea conditions at any time simply by picking up a telephone.

Bad weather isn't necessarily the bogy of sailing; to experienced men it is more a source of discomfort than danger. But as a beginner neither you, nor probably your boat, will yet be prepared to meet it. There is no shame in this; after all the man who has just spent his holiday walking in the Lake District is hardly ready to take on Everest. He needs time to improve his skills, his stamina and his equipment.

Your natural instinct must tell you this but you will probably be a little alarmed by the suggestion that your brand new boat is also unprepared! Let me explain. Undoubtedly the design and hull construction is sound but the boat is still a factory-produced item, with a modest inventory, placed on the market at a competitive price. Taking a boat like this into a gale would be rather like entering the *standard* version of the family car in the East African Safari.

Look around your boat and you will see what I mean. Can you, for example, sleep in rough weather, for it is essential that somebody does? Are there *lee boards* fitted to the bunks to prevent the occupants from being thrown out? Is the interior furniture fitted with retaining clips and hooks; or will you be hit by a barrage of doors and drawers each time the boat rolls?

109

Can you make a hot drink with the boat excessively heeled? Is the stove fitted with gimbals? Will the bilge pump suction still function when the boat is laid on its ear? Do the cockpit drains seem large enough to shed a large amount of water quickly? Do the cabin windows look as if they might stove in? And what about equipment? Do you have storm sails, plenty of oilskins, warps, lifelines and safety harnesses?

And perhaps most important of all, does seasickness knock you for six or can you continue to work through it all? Finally what about your crew? Are they a tough, seasoned band of bluebeards, or is it just mother-in-law, wife, children, teddy-bear and you?

But despite all sensible precautions there is still the chance that you could find yourself several hours away from a port when bad weather strikes, then what do you do? The natural urge is to run for cover but you must temper this with common sense. As has already been shown, the danger in a rough sea is increased with the proximity of land. The harbour you plan to run to may lie in the middle of a lee shore (so what if you should miss?). It may have a dangerous bar in an onshore gale; or it may have a clear entrance exposed to the present wind which would likely make conditions inside untenable. In such circumstances, and if no other port of refuge or anchorage is at hand, then you will have no alternative but to stay out and 'weather the storm'.

Again it is not possible to suggest a definite line of action as this will depend on the boat and the circumstances at the time. However, these are the usual alternatives:

Heaving To

Heaving to is the means by which a boat can be made to stop quietly to keep her steady. It is usually associated with holding up in rough weather but it is also a useful exercise when you need to stop the boat and arrest its wild motion; perhaps to eat, rest or take stock of a situation. The boat is made to heave to by sheeting the jib to windward thus keeping it permanently *backed*, easing the mainsheet, and lashing the tiller downwind. This confounding action takes all way off the boat; the driving force of the wind on the mainsail being counteracted by the

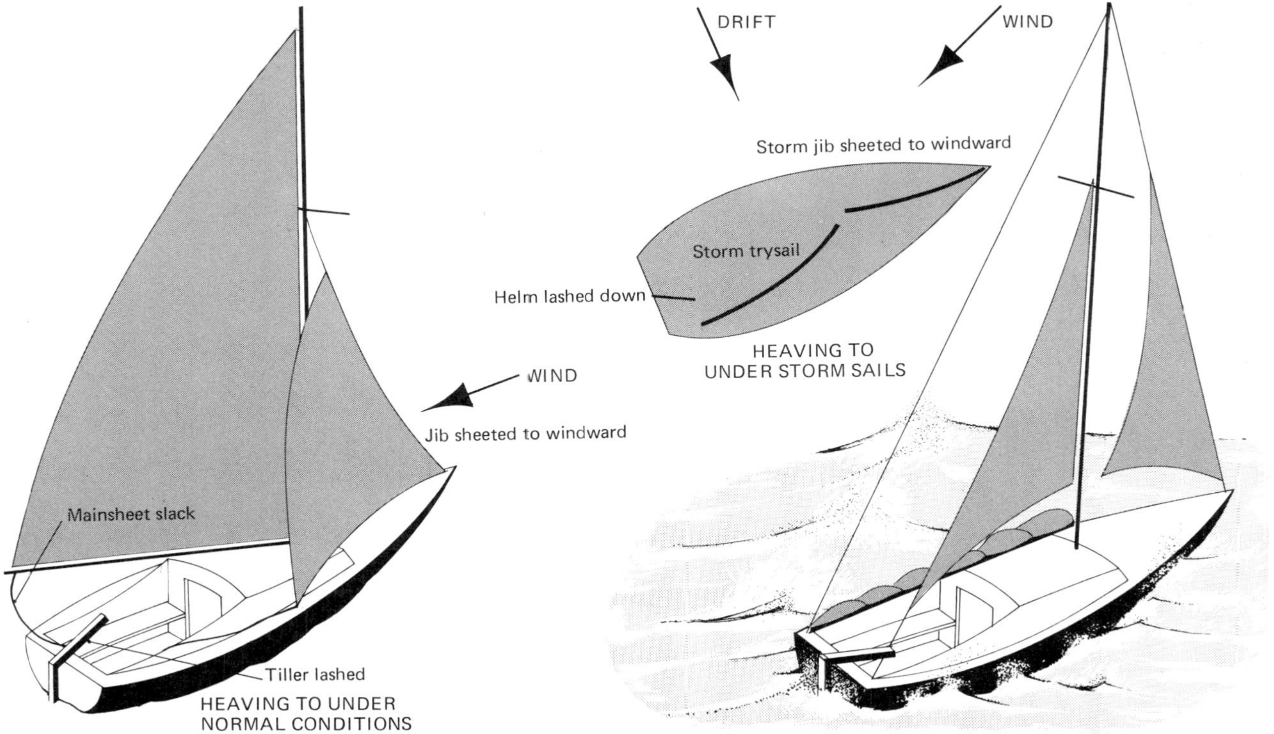

WIND

DRIFT

Storm jib sheeted to windward

Storm trysail

HEAVING TO
UNDER STORM SAILS

Helm lashed down

WIND

Jib sheeted to windward

Mainsheet slack

Tiller lashed

HEAVING TO UNDER
NORMAL CONDITIONS

Fig 22 'Heaving To' i) Heaving to under normal conditions   ii) Heaving to under storm sails

111

tiller and backed jib. In reality the boat does keep moving – she *forereaches* a little and also drifts downwind – but the progress is comparatively slow.

A certain amount of experimentation may be required before the best method of heaving to may be found. Some boats, like the old type of long keel cruising boat will heave to very readily but the more contemporary fin and bilge keel boats may show initial rejection. You may even have to drop one or other of the sails.

Getting to Windward

It is obvious that if you have land behind you it will not be wise to heave to for the boat will, in all probability, drift onto the lee shore. Similarly, and as has already been said, many of the contemporary family cruising boats do not heave to very happily, while in gale conditions it may even be an impossible thing for them to attempt to do. In such circumstances there is no option but to try and get to windward.

If your boat is the typical family cruiser with the benefits of spacious accommodation, standing headroom etc., then unfortunately it will be very difficult for her to make any progress into the wind. The same high and tubby sections of the boat that give you comfortable accommodation now become a disadvantage for it is very much more difficult to drive a shape like this into the wind. Indeed with the sails reefed and the boat heeled there is probably more surface area presented by the body of the boat than there is from the sails – and it is the sails that have to do the work!

The best that can be done in this situation is to try and keep the boat upright, sailing under a jib alone, meeting the seas not head on but on the shoulder which is the safest and most comfortable place for them to be. The boat may make a little progress this way although it will be something if she just holds her own.

Lying a' hull

The one redeeming feature of the family cruiser is her buoyancy and this may be employed, as was suggested before, by getting

112

all the sail off her, lashing the tiller downwind (preferably with a heavy elastic cord to take the strain off the rudder fittings) and *lying a' hull*. In other words leaving the boat to bob along on her own while the crew lies down below. Keep the boat's hatch cover closed to preserve buoyancy and watch for weak spots such as the hatchway and windows.

Running off with Warps

Another alternative, and perhaps one of the most commonly used, is to run before the seas trailing long ropes (mattresses, buckets and similar bulky objects can be tied on the end). These act as a drogue to slow the boat's progress downwind and prevent her from broaching to and being hit sideways on by the waves. The sails, of course, are stowed and this has prompted the alternative term *running under bare poles*. The one disadvantage of this manoeuvre is the risk of being pooped. This is the action of a wave breaking over the stern of a boat to flood the cockpit and perhaps fill the boat. It can, of course, happen whenever a boat is running before a heavy sea but it is more likely to happen when a boat is trailing warps. Once again the family cruiser type is likely to come off worse because of the very much larger cockpits they favour. It means that by retaining a greater quantity and weight of water the boat will lie in a vulnerable position for a longer period with her stern submerged, unable to rise clear of successive waves. For this reason the famly cruising boat would perhaps be safer to lie a' hull rather than risk trailing warps.

14 A FEW MORE THINGS TO KNOW

Next to bed bugs, fog is the worst of all marine hazards, and all the more so for the small boat sailor who is placed at the mercy of big ships which are, in all probability, steaming too fast and with an over-reliance on radar.

Fog can descend quite suddenly, but where you are fore-warned – either by the shipping forecast or, more immediately, by banks of mist or 'breaks' in the sea horizon – then make every possible effort to get out of the shipping lanes and into shallow water where you will be safe. Hoist your radar reflector and try to get a good position check before the fog clamps down.

Once clear of the shipping lanes the most prudent thing to do is to anchor and wait for the fog to clear. However, if you do insist on moving then remember the emphasis on navigation assumes a much greater importance. Unfortunately, with both earthly and heavenly marks denied you, it also becomes very much harder to do. You will need to rely almost exclusively on compass and depth sounder – whatever type that may be – while if you are fortunate enough to have a radio direction finder and a distance log then these will be a great benefit too.

The wind very often dies in fog and your speed will be reduced; in fact this accords very nicely with the Collision Regulations which state that speed *should* be reduced in fog. However, of more relevance is the fact that as you are going slower the influence of the tide on your course will be markedly increased. This is something to bear in mind when navigating and relying largely on an estimate of your position.

Sound becomes vitally important when navigating in fog. If you use an engine then those amongst you with the *best* hearing should stand forward away from the noise and listen for the sound of approaching ships. (If they come very close fire a gun!)

You are, at the same time, obliged to sound your fog signal, an instrument of optional design, although many yachtsmen put a great amount of trust in little trumpets and toot them very authoritatively as if the walls of Jericho might again come tumbling down. In fact they are hopeless. To be heard above the noise of a big ship's engines you need equivalent decibels of a Jumbo jet at take-off or a tom cat crossed in love. I don't know what instrument has this kind of output but as he won't have much else to do at the moment, get the *deafest* man to sound it.

FIRE

The next biggest hazard, and the fact that a boat is completely surrounded by water doesn't seem to help. A boat can be compared to an air-tight container; any combustible fuel, any gas, any vapour that is allowed to spill, leak or weep, can only fall to the bottom of the container, it can never escape. And down in the bottom it poses its greatest threat, for it needs only a chance electrical spark, a match dropped, or a lighted cigarette to ignite it and *Crrump!* the whole thing goes up in smoke. Half a cupful of petrol left in a bilge can be sufficient to blow a boat apart.

Check all fuel, battery and gas installations regularly and scrupulously, make sure that all portable fuel containers are clearly marked – people have been known to try and boil a kettle filled with petrol! When taking fuel aboard extinguish all fires and cigarettes, shut ports and hatches and mop up any spillage the moment it occurs.

Carry at least one or more extinguishers (CO_2, foam or Dry Powder are best) and also a smothering blanket to use in the event of small galley fires. See that everybody aboard knows where the extinguishers are and how to use them. Remember, it is important to get the extinguishers as close to the seat of the fire as possible. Where practical try to prevent further oxygen feeding the fire by shutting all ports and hatches – you may reduce the draught by sailing downwind. Finally, the fore-hatch is your emergency escape in the event of a fire, think very carefully about buying a boat that hasn't been provided with one.

This is one of the fundamental drills for dinghy sailors and something they should practise so they will know precisely how to act and not be nervous if and when the real thing occurs. Most often when a sailing dinghy is first capsized she will lie on her side with her sails resting flat on the water. The first job then is to keep her like this and prevent her from turning right over. Assuming that the crew have already donned life-jackets and have previously lashed all loose items of gear to prevent them floating away, have one man stand on the top of the centre plate (close to the hull where there is no danger of snapping it off) while somebody else ties a life-jacket, or some other form of flotation at the top of the mast. This will then prevent the boat turning turtle. Make sure, however, that the life-jacket is secured to a halyard at the top of the mast so that it may be hauled down later.

The next job is to get the sails down so they will not belly full of water and prevent the boat being pulled upright. The jib can simply be wrapped around the forestay, but the mainsail will probably have to be lowered and either tied or bundled around the boom. The man standing on the centre plate can now grip his fingers around the gunwale and by leaning back should be able to pull the boat upright. (Some people prefer to pass a rope around the mid-section of the boat and lean back on that.)

Once the boat is upright she can be held steady and counter-balanced by one man in the water while the other scrambles aboard over the stern and begins to bucket or splash the water out.

MAN OVERBOARD

The recommended action is to gybe immediately; throw a life-buoy over the side (if you possibly can without wasting too much time) and post somebody who must do nothing else but watch the position of the man in the water. Memorize this drill so that it becomes instinctive; it is far better to react positively and immediately rather than waste precious time figuring out a better manoeuvre.

The purpose of gybing when either close-hauled or on a reach is so that the boat is straight away taken downwind of the man. And it is absolutely vital that the boat should be downwind so that it can then turn and come *upwind* to pick him up. It is virtually impossible and certainly very risky to attempt to pick anything out of the water (man or a mooring buoy) with the wind blowing you down on him.

Because of his weight and the absence of a foothold for him to help himself, it can be extremely difficult to lift a man out of the water. The sensible thing, if it seems that it might be a struggle, is to first pass a bowline over his head and shoulders and secure him to the boat. (There is a story of one wife, clever girl, who finding her husband too heavy to haul aboard, secured him to the boat and sailed him into shallow water where she grounded him.) Once secured you will be able to compose yourself and sort out a solution. One suggestion is that a bight of a wire rope, or a bowline suitably weighted, might be passed over the side for the man to use as a foothold. Alternatively, the main halyard could be secured to his 'lifeline' and he could be heaved aboard on the winch. You may even get him aboard by unhanking the mainsail, dropping the middle part of it over the side and floating him into the belly. Once having netted him in this way you can heave him up on the main halyard. But perhaps an even better suggestion is to launch the inflatable dinghy, if you have one, and get him to climb into that.

But remember the misery, anxiety and discomfort could have all been prevented if, in a cruising boat, the man had been wearing a safety harness attached to a lifeline. It is particularly important that cruiser crews should wear a safety harness and ensure that they are securely attached both in rough weather, when it may be difficult to put the boat about, and on all occasions at night. I cannot over-emphasize the seriousness of a man overboard situation where he may be very quickly lost from view or, in our climate, suffer or die from exposure in a frighteningly short space of time. Do not allow any member of your crew to fool about in a boat nor allow them to lie unwatched on the foredeck or at any time sit with their feet over the side. Warn them also of the danger of filling a bucket of water by trailing it on a line over the side; the drag can easily pluck a man into the water. Finally get into the habit, when walking about the deck of a cruiser, of keeping to the windward side so that if you do slip or get hit by a wave, you fall downhill on the boat, not over the side.

LEAKS

A serious leak, such as might be incurred from hitting something solid, is best tackled by immediately sliding the jib sail, or some other large piece of waterproof material, outside the hull of the boat and positioning it over the hole. The material can be held in place with the aid of ropes while the pressure of water against it should ensure a good seal. It will probably also be necessary to strengthen the inside of the boat by placing floor boards etc. around the vicinity of the hole and shoring them up with dinghy oars, boathooks or any suitable length timber. Cmdr Bill King kept the Indian Ocean out of his boat *Galway Blazer* for an entire fortnight like this after a whale had butted him.

Small leaks can effectively be cured by slapping grease, soap, or even butter over them. While an old recipe that some people swear by is a mixture of sawdust, tar and horse dung. But these ingredients are not easily come by nowadays – and you may have a job persuading the horse of the emergency. The advantage of these cures is that they can be applied on the inside of the boat. Leaky seams on a wooden boat can be plugged from the outside. According to Bernard Moitessier, the French single-handed sailor, the trick is to dive overboard with a tin of sawdust – although be careful, he warns, to hold the tin inverted, otherwise the contents will float out. When you have reached the area of the offending seam, turn the tin the right way up and allow the sawdust to float out and bury itself in the seam above. You may have to assist it by rubbing it into the seams with your fingers but once lodged it will be held by the pressure of water until it swells and fills the gap.

The undoubted best method is a new product called Damage Control Gear which consists of an object, something like an umbrella, which is thrust through the hole from the inside, opened, and pinned back by the pressure of water.

If, in spite of all this the boat fills with water and sinks, then the cardinal rule is stay with her. Few boats actually sink altogether; a wooden boat has the inherent buoyancy of the material; a pocket of air will inevitably become trapped within a glass fibre boat and keep her afloat while a dinghy will have her buoyancy bags (won't she?). Do not try to swim for the shore unless it is literally within spitting distance. Distances at sea are remarkably deceptive and besides, even if the shore 'appears' to be close, there may be a very strong tidal stream to contend with. But apart from these considerations it must be borne in mind that your boat will make a far better marker for your rescuers to find, far better than a head bobbing in the water anyway!

One final reason for staying with the boat is that if the water is cold – which if around the British Isles it is certain to be – then it is essential to restrict your movements as much as possible to conserve body heat. For this reason too, put on as many clothes as are practical before you are forced into the water.

GOING AGROUND

This is more of a problem for cruisers. If size and circumstances permit, the best way to get her re-floated is for the crew to jump over-side and push. Make sure that one person stays aboard to handle the boat when she is freed, otherwise you will move into an even worse situation. It is important that the engine is shut off and that all the pushers wear life-jackets. The second best method is to induce a list (this doesn't apply to bilge keel boats) and so reduce the boat's draft. Lower the mainsail, secure the topping lift to the main boom, have one or two men drape themselves over it and then swing it as far outboard as it will go. Alternatively, the boat's draft may be reduced overall if all the crew stand forward.

Other suggestions include 'lightening ship' by having all but one person take to the dinghy or by making the boat roll from side to side while the engine is put in reverse. Although if you had been able to put the boat on to the other tack the moment she touched she might have come clear immediately and you would have been spared all this trouble.

But no matter what action you take it must be immediate, especially with a falling tide. If you do find yourself *sewed*, or stuck on the mud until the following high tide, it is important to lay out a kedge anchor. This is a second and usually smaller anchor which, with its rope warp, is more portable. Its purpose here is to hold the boat in position – although you may hardly think this necessary since the boat is pretty solidly stuck where she is. However unless the boat is held steady the succeeding tide would do no more than lift her while the wind or the waves pushed her ashore again. The kedge anchor prevents this.

It may either be walked out in the direction of the deep water or it can be taken out and dropped from the dinghy. If you do have to row the kedge anchor out be sure to coil the warp in the dinghy rather than have somebody try to feed it to you from on board. Make sure also that the warp is clear to run when you drop the anchor otherwise you might go down with it. Once the anchor has been dropped, or satisfactorily buried, heave in the slack from on board the boat and make fast. The boat will then be ready to heave clear when the water returns giving you sufficient time to start the engine or hoist the sails.

Kedging is another very useful way to refloat a boat in the early stages of grounding when with the back up of a good winch or a strong crew the boat can often be pulled clear of the mud.

ANCHORING

Apart from providing the boat with its 'brake' (although a bucket thrown over the side on a length of rope can slow a boat quite effectively), an anchor is used to secure the boat to the earth, either for a few hours while a tide serves, or for quite an extended period. However, for the anchor to hold the boat securely, certain conditions must be met. The waters should be reasonably calm or sheltered; the sea bed should be composed of a good holding material and the chart will indicate this (rocks, or loose shingle for example make a poor holding ground) and the amount of cable veered must be at least three times the depth of water – at high water also!

You should not anchor in a main channel, nor even close to it if there is a danger that you will swing with the tide and create an obstruction; nor should you anchor near a buoy nor close enough to obscure it from others, while it is also forbidden to anchor close over a telegraph or underwater electricity cable, or obviously too near any other anchored boats.

To anchor a boat first position her so that she faces the wind or tide, whichever is the stronger (the direction in which the other anchored boats are lying may give you a clue). Steer the boat some way ahead of where you actually wish to lie and stop her. Drop the anchor gently on the sea bed and check the cable so that it doesn't all fall into a heap on top of the anchor. Allow the boat to drift astern and as she does, slack away more cable so that it is laid along the sea bed. When sufficient cable has been veered make it fast. It will be necessary to ensure at the earliest opportunity that the anchor is not dragging. This can be found either by watching objects in line on the shore or by lowering the weighted sounding line onto the bottom and watching to see if the line moves. Remember that the Collision Regulations compel you to show an anchor signal which is a large black ball aloft in the forepart of the boat during the daytime and a light in the same place at night.

REEFING

Sailing boats are designed, naturally enough, to sail in all kinds of winds. However, to do this efficiently they need both to be able to increase their sail area when the wind is light and reduce it when the wind is strong. To reduce the foresail area is easy, you simply select a smaller sail (most cruising boats will carry three foresails: a *storm jib*, a *working jib* and a *Genoa*). But the mainsail you are stuck with and the only way to reduce the area of this is by taking a temporary tuck in at the bottom. At least that's what it is in dressmaking terms, sailors call it *reefing*.

There are two common methods of reefing: one is the older *slab* reefing where the sail is lashed to the boom with reef points, and the other is *roller* reefing in which the sail is wound round the boom. Some boats have a combination of both. Although the technique varies with each, the aims are the same; the reefed sail must retain its proper shape which means stretching the leach well aft as the reef is put in and also securing the

121

topping lift before you start so that the weight of the boom is supported.

The reef is begun with the sail hoisted. If it is roller reefing then the main halyard is slacked the equivalent to one roll at a time and the sail-slides eased from the mast track. The leach is stretched back and the sail battens removed as their pockets are rolled. At all times keep the mainsheet slack so that sail and boom will feather in the wind.

Ideally, a reef is put in before you begin sailing, at least if the weather demands, but you can just as easily reef while under way. Luff up into the wind, let go the mainsheet and the tiller and the boat should reach quite happily under her jib until the operation is complete.

Weather forecast and present wind strength apart – and do realize the importance of reefing early before conditions make it too difficult or before damage is done – you will very soon know by the 'feel' of the boat when a reef is needed. She becomes more difficult to control, heels excessively, is increasingly wet, while the amount of weather helm makes her hard to hold. In short she is unbalanced.

You will be amazed how much more comfortable she will be when reefed, and surprisingly, with no great sacrifice to speed. Practise it.

HM Coastguard, who have responsibility for co-ordinating sea rescue around our coast, have introduced a helpful scheme for yachtsmen making coastal passages. The principle is that you supply them with details of your boat, her construction, capabilities etc., and at the same time list the ports you plan to call at together with the times you hope to arrive. This information is then passed to the various Coastguard stations along your route who will keep a look out for you. It is important, however, that you should contact the local Coastguard immediately on arrival at each port and indeed it's upon this report that the principle of the scheme depends. Because if you do fail to report and have also failed to notify your 'agent' – a relative or friend whom you have arranged to contact regularly throughout the trip – then the Coastguard will, if the weather has been bad and your boat is particularly small, initiate a search for you.

Provided you are prepared to make these arranged contacts at each port, it is a good scheme and one that will give both you, and your family ashore, a great deal of comfort. For further details telephone your local Coastguard and ask for information of CG66, Coastal Passage Scheme.

USEFUL ADDRESSES

Island Cruising Club, Island Street, Salcombe, Devon.

Lloyds Register of Shipping, Yacht and Small Craft Department, 69, Oxford Street, Southampton so1 1DL.

National Sailing Centre, Arctic Road, Cowes, Isle of Wight.

Ocean Youth Club, 160 Piccadilly, London, w1.

Royal Yachting Association, Victoria Way, Woking, Surrey, GU21 1EQ.

Royal Yachting Association, Membership Office, Shaftesbury Road, Gillingham, Dorset SP8 4LJ.

Sail Training Association, No 3, Glencoe, Bosham Lane, Old Bosham, Chichester, Sussex.

Ship and Boatbuilders' National Federation, 31 Great Queen Street, London, WC2B 5AD.

Sports Council, 70 Brompton Road, London, SW3 1HE.

Yacht Brokers, Designers and Surveyors Association, Orchard Hill, The Avenue, Haslemere, Surrey.

Yacht Charters Association, 33, Highfield Road, Lymington, Hants.

FURTHER READING

Coastal Cruising, Colin Jarman, A. & C. Black Ltd.

Cruising, J. D. Sleightholme, Adlard Coles Ltd.

Navigation for Yachtsmen, Mary Blewitt, Iliffe Books Ltd.

Small Boat Navigation, Lt.-Cdr. Pat Hepherd, Stanley Paul Ltd.

Build Your Own Boat, Percy W. Blandford, Stanley Paul Ltd.

Foam Sandwich Boat Building, Peter Wynn, George Allen & Unwin.

Yachting Monthly and Ferro-Cement, Yachting Monthly, Yachting Monthly Publications.

Boat Building on a Glass Fibre Hull, Dave Gannaway, Nautical Publishing Co.

Start to Win, Eric Twiname, Adlard Coles Ltd.

Make Sail: Build Your Own Boat, Peter Heaton, Pelham Books.

Starting Sailing, James Moore and Alan Turvey, David & Charles.

Sailing from Start to Finish, Yves-Louis Pinaud, Adlard Coles Ltd.

Basic Coastal Navigation, Conrad Dixon, Adlard Coles Ltd.

Instant Weather Forecasting, Alan Watts, Adlard Coles Ltd.

Way of a Yacht, Alan Hollingsworth, David & Charles.

Small Boat Racing, James Moore, Stanley Paul Ltd.

Modern Rope Seamanship, Bill Beavis and Colin Jarman, Adlard Coles Ltd.

INDEX

compiled by Susan Kennedy